The Hong Kong Economic Policy Studies Series

INCOME INEQUALITY
AND
ECONOMIC DEVELOPMENT

T0154856

INCOME INEQUALITY AND ECONOMIC DEVELOPMENT

Hon-Kwong Lui

Published for

The Hong Kong Centre for Economic Research

The Hong Kong Economic Policy Studies Forum

by

City University of Hong Kong Press

First published 1997
Printed in Hong Kong

ISBN 962-937-006-9

Published by
City University of Hong Kong Press
City University of Hong Kong
Tat Chee Avenue, Kowloon, Hong Kong

Internet: http://www.cityu.edu.hk/upress/
E-mail: upress@cityu.edu.hk

The free-style calligraphy on the cover, *jun*, means "*equality*" in Chinese.

Contents

Detailed Chapter Contents

Foreword

The key to the economic success of Hong Kong has been a business and policy environment which is simple, predictable and transparent. Experience shows that prosperity results from policies that protect private property rights, maintain open and competitive markets, and limit the role of the government.

The rapid structural change of Hong Kong's economy in recent years has generated considerable debate over the proper role of economic policy in the future. The impending restoration of sovereignty over Hong Kong from Britain to China has further complicated the debate. Anxiety persists as to whether the pre-1997 business and policy environment of Hong Kong will continue.

During this period of economic and political transition in Hong Kong, various interested parties will be re-assessing Hong Kong's existing economic policies. Inevitably, they will advocate an agenda aimed at altering the present policy making framework to reshape the future course of public policy.

For this reason, it is of paramount importance for those familiar with economic affairs to reiterate the reasons behind the success of the economic system in the past, to identify what the challenges are for the future, to analyze and understand the economy sector by sector, and to develop appropriate policy solutions to achieve continued prosperity.

In a conversation with my colleague Y. F. Luk, we came upon the idea of inviting economists from universities in Hong Kong to take up the challenge of examining systematically the economic policy issues of Hong Kong. An expanding group of economists (The Hong Kong Economic Policy Studies Forum) met several times to give form and shape to our initial ideas. The Hong Kong Economic Policy Studies Project was then launched in 1996 with some 30 economists from the universities in Hong Kong and a few from overseas. This is the first time in Hong Kong history that a concerted public effort has been undertaken by academic economists in the territory. It represents a joint expression of our collective concerns, our hopes for a better Hong Kong, and our faith in the economic future.

The Hong Kong Centre for Economic Research is privileged to be co-ordinating this Project. The unfailing support of many distinguished citizens in our endeavour and their words of encouragement are especially gratifying. We also thank the directors and editors of the City University of Hong Kong Press and The Commercial Press (H.K.) Ltd. for their enthusiasm and dedication which extends far beyond the call of duty.

> Yue-Chim Richard Wong
> Director
> The Hong Kong Centre
> for Economic Research

Foreword by Series Editor

The economic performance of Hong Kong has been phenomenal, and the good record has long been acknowledged throughout the world. Hong Kong has bootstrapped itself from the ranks of developing economies to be high on the list of the developed ones.

In comparison, changes in the population characteristics of Hong Kong have received much less attention. Due to the high degree of freedom both of emigration and immigration, to high life expectancy, and to low fertility — in part caused by economic development — there have been rapid changes in the size and structure of the population and the labour force. Yet, how many people in Hong Kong get to reap the harvest of its economic success? How much do they share? To appreciate Hong Kong's economic performance, we should not focus only on the total economic output; we should also know about the pattern of income distribution among the people.

As an economy undergoes drastic transformation, there are always people who are unable to adjust well or to adjust fast enough. They are left in the lower end of income distribution and they feel more and more deprived (relative to other people). Under the current policy environment in Hong Kong, they are more ready than ever before to express their dissatisfaction, either directly or indirectly, in order to exert pressure on economic policy-making. Since personal interests are involved, it is quite often that discussions on income distribution are emotionally loaded. However, when it comes to designing policies, it is imperative to avoid partiality and emotions as much as we can.

Income distribution is the outcome of interactions between factors of many dimensions: economic, sociological, educational, and political. It is no easy task to clearly delineate the causes and effects of income inequality. Unfortunately, a complicated matter like this tends to be condensed to some figures (such as the Gini coefficient), while discussions and even policy proposals are often based purely on such abstract figures. It is quite obvious that a lot of details could be missed.

What are the commonly used measures or indicators of income distribution. What kinds of scientific connotation do they carry? What is the current situation of income distribution in Hong Kong, as measured by such indicators. How has it changed over time. Have certain important government policies been able to bring about a more equal income distribution?

This book addresses these questions in detail, and the arguments are based on careful data analysis. The author, Dr. Hon-kwong Lui, first introduces the meaning and indicators of income distribution, and then describes the changing pattern of income distribution in Hong Kong as the economy develops. He also compares the income distribution of different sociological groups, such as male versus female employees, local residents versus immigrants from Mainland China, and public housing residents versus tenants in private housing.

As education and housing are the two most important items in the list of government expenditures, and since these two can have a bearing on income distribution, Dr. Lui carries out a quantitative analysis of an important policy question: Whether and how education and housing policies may affect income distribution in Hong Kong.

Dr. Lui's main research interests include the labour market and income distribution in Hong Kong. He is familiar with handling massive amounts of detailed census data. His study contributes a lot to our understanding of various aspects of Hong Kong's income distribution. The book is a good reference for the discussion and design of fiscal and related public polices.

Y. F. Luk
School of Economics and Finance
The University of Hong Kong

Preface

I am grateful to two anonymous referees for many useful and detailed comments. I benefited from discussions with Wing Suen and Richard Wong. Mon Ho of the Hong Kong Centre for Economic Research offered efficient and timely logistical support. I would like to thank the Finance Branch, Government Secretariat of the Hong Kong Government for providing statistical data for Table 4.1 and Figure 4.1. (Financial support to be filled by the HKCER.) The emotional support I receive from my wife, Veronica, has always been invaluable to me.

Hon-Kwong Lui
Department of Marketing
and International Business
Lingnan College
Hong Kong

List of Illustrations

Figures

Tables

Income Inequality
and
Economic Development

CHAPTER 1

Introduction

The economy of Hong Kong grew at a rapid pace in the last few decades. The economic restructuring has transformed the nature of the economy successfully. Hong Kong has grown from a trading port (entrepôt) to a manufacturing centre and subsequently to a regional hub of services. As Hong Kong becomes increasingly prosperous, the income dispersion of families widens. The income inequality problem has aroused more and more public attention. Researchers have different views on the issue of heightened income inequality in Hong Kong. Tsang (1993) argues that there has been a long-term trend of increasing income dispersion in the city, and he believes that the China-link might cause income levels to grow even more disparate in the foreseeable future. On the other hand, Chau's (1994) analysis does not indicate that relative income distributions has become more of a problem after 1971. He suggests that the fruits of economic progress have trickled down to all income levels, and that there has been extensive upward mobility of low-income households, particularly since the late 1970s.

If we look at Table 1.1, we can observe that during the period from 1976 to 1991 the economy was moving towards greater inequality in both household and personal income distribution. Among many measures of income inequality, the Gini coefficient is the most widely used index.[1] The Gini coefficient takes a value between zero and one. The higher is the value of Gini coefficient, the greater is the level of income dispersion, and by implication, income inequality. The official Gini coefficient of household income rose from 0.430 in 1976 to 0.518 in 1996 (Column B), whereas the Gini

Table 1.1

Gini Coefficient for Hong Kong

Year	Gini Coefficient			
	Household Income (A)	Household Income (B)	Household Income (C)	Personal Earnings (D)
1957	0.480	–	–	–
1966	0.487	–	0.467	–
1971	0.443	0.430	0.409	–
1976	0.435	0.430	0.409	0.386
1981	0.433	0.451	0.453	0.382
1986	0.437	0.453	–	0.410
1991	0.431	0.476	–	0.427
1996		0.518	–	–

Sources:
(A) Chau (1994)
(B) Census Statistics Department (1978, 1993, 1996c)
(C) Lin (1985)
(D) Suen (1995)

coefficient of personal earnings increased from 0.386 to 0.427 (Column D) in the period from 1976 to 1991. In fact, the level of income inequality in Hong Kong was among the highest in Asia and the Pacific (Deininger and Squire 1996) during this period. There is legitimate reason for the widespread concern about increased income inequality. The present book documents the relationship between income distribution and economic growth. Income distribution is analyzed from different perspectives. The impact of education and public housing policies on income distribution is also discussed.

The gross domestic product (GDP) per capita of Hong Kong (at current market prices) rose from HK$2,300 in 1961 to HK$179,600 in 1995, increasing close to 80 times (Census & Statistics Department 1996a).[2] In real term, GDP per capita (at constant 1990 market prices) rose from HK$19,500 in 1961 to HK$122,900 in 1995. In other words, real per capita income increased 5.3 times in 34 years, representing an annual growth rate of 5.6%.

The total population and the labour force of Hong Kong also grew rapidly. The territory's population doubled in thirty years, going from 3.2 million in 1961 to 6.2 million in 1996. The labour force grew in size from 1.2 million in 1961 to 2.9 million in 1996. Accommodating the large increase in the population, not to mention creating 1.7 million jobs for the extra members of the workforce, proved a serious challenge for policy makers. Fortunately, during these years the economy was growing at such a rapid rate that instead of resulting in massive unemployment, there were at times labour shortage in selected sectors of the economy.

In addition to worrying about employment levels and economic growth, the public is particularly concerned about the rate of the change in price level. In Hong Kong, the consumer price index (A), which covers 50% of all households in the economy, is generally used as a proxy measure of inflation. However, the "GDP deflator" is a better indicator of price changes in relation to goods and services produced in the economy. From 1961 to 1995 the GDP deflator rose more than twelve-fold, which is equivalent to an annual inflation rate of 7.6% (Census & Statistics Department 1996a). Hong Kong residents had little difficulty adapting to this sustained and high level of inflation, though, because real wage rates increased proportionally during the same period. Wong et al. (1991) argue that the high rate of inflation is partly attributable to rapid economic transformation.

In the literature, there are many studies that deal with the relationship between inflation and income distribution. For example, Newbery (1995) shows that changes in relative prices do not appear to be correlated with distributional characteristics. He argues that experiences in Hungary and the U.K. indicate that relative price changes have no adverse effect on the distribution of purchasing power. This book, however, does not discuss the main causes of inflation or the relationship between inflation and income distribution.[3]

Several stages of economic transformations have led to substantial shift in employment patterns, i.e. "sectoral shifts". Skills which commanded high wages in the past are obsolete today. For

Table 1.2
Average Gini Coefficient for Selected Regions in the World

Region	Gini Coefficient in the	
	1960s	1990s
Latin America and the Caribbean	0.532	0.493
Sub-Saharan Africa	0.499	0.470
Middle East and North Africa	0.414	0.380
East Asia and the Pacific	0.374	0.381
South Asia	0.362	0.319
Industrial countries and high-income developing countries	0.350	0.338
Eastern Europe	0.251	0.289

Source: Deininger and Squire (1996)

example, many workers employed in the clothing industry in the early eighties have found their skills and experience useless in the mid-nineties. The growing importance of the service economy suggests a general upgrading in labour demand. If economic restructuring at such a rapid pace were to occur in another economy, economists would anticipate a widespread mismatch between employment opportunities and the skills of the unemployed. However, the labour market in Hong Kong has adjusted smoothly to changes in demand, and the employment rate has remained at a very high level by international standards. Although persistent and acute structural unemployment has not been a big problem in Hong Kong, wages of workers are becoming increasingly disparate.

There is little doubt that Hong Kong's economic transformation has benefited the majority of local workers, especially those who are better educated. However, two groups of people, the less educated and the elderly, may suffer more than other groups as a result of the changes. Suen (1995) suggests that there is evidence that workers with no education are at a relative disadvantage when competing with other workers. Yet, there is no evidence to support the view that the wage gap between older workers and younger workers has widened.

How has economic restructuring affected income distribution in Hong Kong's economy as a whole? Whereas the United Nations categorizes Hong Kong as a developing economy, the World Bank classifies it as a high-income economy. According to the *World Development Report 1995* published by the World Bank, Hong Kong has the highest rate of income inequality among high-income economies. Table 1.2 summarizes the average Gini coefficient for selected regions in the world in the 1960s and the 1990s. In the 1990s the average Gini coefficient for East Asia and the Pacific was 0.38, which is much higher than the corresponding figures for industrial and high-income developing economies. From Table 1.1, we can see that the Gini coefficient for Hong Kong stood at 0.48 in 1991. Apparently, the distribution of household income in Hong Kong at that time was highly unequal by international standards.

The relationship between income distribution and economic growth has been a popular topic among academics and politicians (see, for example, Mincer 1970, and Nickell and Bell 1996). The issue of whether rapid economic growth causes inequality in income distribution to increase has yet to be resolved. However, Nobel Laureate Gary S. Becker (1995) argues that income inequality may be an engine that drives an economy toward faster economic growth.

Economic Growth and Income Distribution

In general, economic growth benefits an economy as a whole by creating more jobs and improving the standard of living. It is logical to ask whether all households and individuals share equally in the fruits of economic growth. In a seminal paper, another Nobel Laureate Simon Kuznets (1955), proposes that income inequality in a country widens in the early phases of economic development; as the economy continues to develop, however, income dispersion narrows mainly because of a general rise in the proportion of middle-income families. In other words, he suggests that income distribution follows an inverted U-curve. His theory is often referred to as Kuznet's inverted-U hypothesis.

Recent empirical evidence concerning Kuznets' hypothesis is inconclusive (Chang 1994).[4] Some studies found that inequality has a negative effect on economic growth. For example, Persson and Tabellini (1994) develop a theoretical model and argue that inequality is harmful for growth. They suggest that this relationship is only present in democracies, and that government policies and political forces can induce a negative correlation between income inequality and economic growth.

The relationship between income distribution and economic growth in Hong Kong has aroused the interest of numerous researchers. For example, Chow's (1977) doctoral dissertation examines the trend and patterns in (1) the distribution of income and (2) changes in the absolute income of the poor in Hong Kong from the 1950s to the early 1970s. In a report prepared for the International Labour Office, Hsia and Chau (1978) assess the impact of Hong Kong's industrialization on income distribution. Lin (1985) analyzes the government's income redistribution policies, and Lam (1995) studies the way in which income distribution has been affected by mass immigration from China.

In Hong Kong, the government regularly publishes the Gini coefficient in population censuses. Table 1.1 shows four sets of Gini coefficients for Hong Kong for the period 1957–1996. These coefficients are computed by the government and three researchers.[5] Since these Gini coefficients are derived from different data sets using different methods, they should not be used for direct comparison. These series are included here to show the overall trend.

Kuznets' conjecture is not supported well by Hong Kong's experience. In the initial stage of the economic development, income distribution was relatively unequal, and the Gini coefficient was 0.467 in 1966 (Column C). Industrialization in the 1970s brought about greater equality. When Hong Kong moved into the third wave (service economy) in the 1980s, the Gini coefficient (Column B in Table 1.1) of household income distribution increased from 0.451 in 1981 to 0.518 in 1996. The personal earnings distribution shown in Column D of Table 1.1 tells essentially the same story. There has been a greater rise of income distribution inequality. The Gini coefficient for male employment earnings rose from 0.386 in 1976 to 0.427 in 1991. Looking at these figures, one may jump to the rash conclusion that economic restructuring in Hong Kong has caused an overall increase in inequality. Although this is highly possible, the causal relationship cannot be established lightly.

Government Policies and Income Distribution

Hong Kong is a world-renowned *laissez-faire* economy that has experienced rapid economic growth in the post-war period. Government intervention has always been kept to a minimum; capital can flow freely in and out. The taxation system is very simple, and the tax burdens of individuals and corporations have remained light by international standards. The ratio of government expenditure to GDP is among the lowest in the world. Government spending has always constituted less than one-fifth of the GDP. Nobel Laureate Milton Friedman has described Hong Kong as the last frontier of free trade economy. Thus, Hong Kong provides an interesting testing ground for Kuznets' hypothesis concerning effects of economic growth in general, and, in particular for hypotheses concerning effects of public policies upon income inequality of an economy.

More than 40% of all households in Hong Kong reside in public housing units. Public housing refers to rental blocks provided by the Housing Authority and Housing Society, as well as to living quarters in home-ownership estates. Since rents charged by the government are well below market value, there is always a long list of applicants who meet all public housing requirements awaiting allocation of these flats. Households living in public housing receive heavy subsidies from the government. This should be taken into account in measuring income distribution of individuals and households in Hong Kong.

It is almost universally agreed that education is an important form of human capital and that highly educated workers earn more than less-educated ones do. Moreover, education can increase one's upward social mobility. In the past, tuition fees were very high and university education and, to a lesser extent, secondary education was restricted to children from families with a high social and economic status. The implementation of a nine-year free and compulsory education policy in 1978 was a giant step taken by the government to improve the general educational level as well as the earning power of Hong Kong residents. It is now a government policy that students should not be turned away from universities because of inability to pay. Recently, the government also increased the availability of tertiary education in Hong Kong. The government aims at providing enough first-year, first-degree places to accommodate 18% of youngsters aged seventeen to twenty. Although the full impact of this ambitious expansion plan has yet to be felt, it is likely that the expansion would significantly benefit lower-income families. For decades, children from higher-income families prefer to further their university studies abroad. Children from lower-income families cannot afford that, and those who are not admitted to any local tertiary institution would receive no tertiary education. The government's plan aims to rectify this situation.

We should consider government social services when studying income distribution. Broadly speaking, social services can be divided into two main components: health care services and social welfare services.[6] In Hong Kong, medical and health care services provided in public hospitals and clinics are heavily subsidized by the government, or more correctly speaking, by taxpayers. Medical consultation is available to the general public at a nominal fee, and this consultation fee also covers prescriptions. Free child health services are provided for local residents. A comprehensive immunization programme is available free of charge for newborns and primary school students.

Although Hong Kong does not provide comprehensive unemployment or retirement benefits to individuals, it is incorrect to say that the government ignores the unemployed or the elderly. The government provides financial assistance to the disadvantaged through social security schemes such as a social security allowance, emergency relief, traffic accident victims assistance, and comprehensive social security assistance. For example, in the 1994–1995 fiscal year, the government distributed HK$3,427 million to 109,461 successful applicants to the comprehensive social security assistance scheme (Census & Statistics Department 1995). On average, each applicant received HK$31,000 from the government. Apparently, this kind of direct government transfer affects the overall distribution of income. In short, the effects of various government policies should be taken into consideration in calculating indices of income inequality in Hong Kong.

On 1 July 1997 the People's Republic of China will resume its sovereignty over Hong Kong. Under the Basic Law, offsprings of Hong Kong citizens who are living in China will then have the right to migrate to Hong Kong. Although the government does not have an accurate estimate of the number of persons who are eligible to come to Hong Kong under this agreement, that number is likely to be very large. Throughout Hong Kong's history, immigrants from China have constituted a significant portion of the territory's population. In 1911 Chinese immigrants accounted for more than 60% of Hong Kong's population (Fan 1974). In 1974 Hong Kong introduced various policies to restrict the influx of Chinese immigrants. At the time of this writing (early 1997), a daily maximum of 150 Chinese immigrants are allowed into Hong Kong. Various studies (see, for example, Lam 1996 and Lui and Suen 1996) have found that Chinese immigrants to Hong Kong earn much less than native workers do. The number of immigrants from China thus clearly affects overall income distribution (see Lam 1996 for further discussion). Since the number of Chinese immigrants allowed to reside in Hong Kong is affected by the government's immigration policy, immigration policy in itself becomes a determinant of Hong Kong's overall income distribution.

The Scope of this Study

This book analyzes the temporal changes in the distribution of income in Hong Kong among individuals and among households. The redistributive impact of education and public housing policies in Hong Kong is also analyzed. In the next chapter, I present stylized facts about Hong Kong's economic growth during the past few decades. Economic restructuring has led to a substantial reallocation of labour across sectors. The chapter documents the pattern of sectoral shifts of the labour force and assesses the effects of such shifts on the distribution of income. Chapter 3 discusses the changes in income distribution. I describe the data sets used in this study and present the empirical results. In addition to the Gini coefficient, different measures of income inequality are introduced and analyzed. In Chapter 4, the relationship between the government's education policy and income distribution is examined. I focus on the major changes in the education policy and to their effects on income distribution. The housing policy and its redistributive effects are also analyzed in Chapter 4. In estimating the pattern of income distribution, I employ two simple methods to take into account the benefits received by households living in public housing. The concluding chapter summarizes the results of this study.

Notes

1. Cowell (1995) provides a comprehensive survey of different techniques for measuring income distribution. He also discusses the theoretical and practical problems involved in measuring inequality. See Chapter 3 for further discussion of some income inequality measures.

2. Since 17 October 1983 the Hong Kong dollar has been linked to the U.S. dollar at a fixed exchange rate of HK$7.80 = US$1.00.

3. For those interested in the reasons behind the persistent high inflation rate, please see A. Siu (forthcoming) in this Series.

4. See Adelman and Robinson (1989) for a survey of the research on the relationship between economic development and income distribution. See also Anand and Kanbur (1993) for another example of a study of the question raised by Kuznets.

5. The longest series in the table (Column A) is extracted from Chau (1994). Data in Column B are official figures published by the government, and data in Column C are computed by Lin (1985). Statistics in columns A to

C are Gini coefficients of household income distribution. The figures in Column D refer to the Gini coefficient of personal earnings distribution calculated by Suen (1995). Suen's data files are the 1% random samples of unpublished census files, and he only selects working men in his analysis.

6. A separate book prepared by L. S. Ho (forthcoming) in this Series analyzes the delivery and financing of health care services.

CHAPTER 2

Economic Growth, Sectoral Shifts, and Income Distribution

Distribution of Income: A Brief Review

There is a great deal of literature discussing personal and household income distributions. Sahota (1978), for example, provides a useful survey of general theories of personal income distribution, while Mincer (1970) focuses on the application of the human capital approach to the analysis of personal income distribution. Other relevant studies include Borjas (1990), Simon (1989), and Stark (1991). These studies try to determine the impact of immigrants on the distribution of income. There is no clear evidence to support the view that the inflow of immigrants increases income disparity. Simon (1989) argues that immigrants can narrow income dispersion in the long run.

Various socioeconomic variables may affect the distribution of income, and they are frequently used to analyze income disparity. Scholars, notably economists, are keen to provide explanations for observed income inequality. For instance, Cole and Towe (1996) indicate that changes in family structure and demographics are major contributors to the increasingly disparate income levels of U.S. residents. Jenkins (1995) argues that changes in age distribution and household composition are important in explaining rising income disparity in the U.K. Among the socioeconomic variables, gender arouses the most debates by academics and the public (see, for example, Gunderson 1989, Rosenfeld and Kalleberg 1990). In different parts of the world, we observe pervasive and significant gender earnings gaps. Blau and Kahn (1992) compare the gender income differential of several industrialized countries. Researchers are also interested in the role of women in the distribution of household income. Smith (1979) and Danziger (1980) point out that working wives make household income distribution more equal.

In addition to attributing income inequality to demographic changes, researchers often try to establish the relationship between economic growth, or economic transformation, and income disparity. Studies on the relationship between economic growth and income distribution originated in the seminal work of Kuznets (1955). He suggests that income inequality increases in the early stages of an economy's development, after which income distribution stabilized. Income distribution subsequently grows more equal when the economy continues to develop. A simplified version of his argument is that when an economy begins to develop, people move from rural to urban areas. As level of income dispersion in rural areas is lower than that in cities, overall income distribution should be more unequal at this early stages of development. As the economy continues to grow, education becomes widely available and reduces the differential in returns to schooling. Hence, income distribution will be more equal later on. However, empirical evidence has yet to establish the exact relationship between economic growth and income inequality.

Becker (1995) argues that greater income inequality may be an engine for faster economic growth. However, Persson and Tabellini (1994) propose that inequality is harmful to growth in democratic societies. Their theoretical analysis indicates that income inequality leads to policies that do not protect property rights and do not allow full private appropriation of returns from investment. Moreover, Haslag et al. (1988) study the two-way interactions between growth and inequality. They use the case of Mexico to determine whether economic growth "causes" income inequality or whether inequality "leads" to economic growth. They conclude that growth does promote greater equality in the distribution of economic welfare. Moreover, the data do not support the view that changes in the distribution of income cause changes in the rate of economic growth. Birdsall et al. (1995) show that East Asian economies have experienced rapid economic growth coupled with relatively low levels of income disparity.

Sectoral shifts in employment have also been identified as an important cause of rising income disparity. The literature on this topic is extensive, and I only briefly outline some findings on the relationship between sectoral shifts and inequality. Some researchers find evidence to support the view that sectoral shifts are one of the causes of rising inequality. For example, Lawrence (1984) suggests that sectoral shifts in employment were one of the factors, though not the most important one, affecting the distribution of earnings in the U.S. during the period 1969 to 1983. However, Grubb and Wilson (1989) argue that increasing inequality within various occupational groups and sectors was responsible for most of the increasing inequality between 1960 and 1980. Other researchers cast doubt on the relationship between sectoral shifts and rising income inequality. Howell (1995) states that there is little direct evidence to support the idea of a pervasive and persistent mismatch of skills, even when there have been substantial shifts in the occupational mix of employment. Leonard and Jacobson (1990) study industrial restructuring in Pennsylvania between 1974 and 1987. Despite the fact that nearly one-third of all manufacturing jobs were eliminated during the period, the earnings distribution remained largely unchanged. They conclude that industrial restructuring has no adverse affect on earnings distribution.

In their search for an explanation for rising income inequality in the U.S., economists have shifted their focus from economic restructuring to other variables. Bluestone (1990) argues that increasing returns to schooling coupled with sectoral shifts are responsible for the increase in wage dispersion. Juhn et al. (1993) analyze the effects of changing industrial composition on wage inequality. They suggest that sectoral shifts and changes in the occupation composition influence wage inequality but only minimally. They argue that the trend toward increased wage inequality is attributable to the rise in returns to skill. In a recent study, Blau and Kahn (1996) highlight the importance of institutions in explaining wage inequality. They find that wage centralization is negatively associated with wage dispersion. In Hong Kong, wage-setting institutions are virtually nonexistent. If Blau and Kahn's hypothesis is correct, Hong Kong should experience higher income dispersion than do other economies, holding other factors constant.

Redistributive Policies and Income Distribution

Uneven distribution of income is a social problem of national interest. Chang (1994) suggests that extreme inequality is widely considered a major cause of political instability and even civil war. Governments are frequently asked to combat income inequality. Scholars and governments repeatedly pose one question: Is there a trade-off between augmenting economic growth and reducing income inequality? Public policies aimed at reducing inequality may provide negative incentives for economic efficiency (Chang 1994). Browning (1989) argues that the promotion of equality through public policies has gone too far. He states that while helping the truly needy is unobjectionable, extending policies to permit redistribution among the general population is often counter- productive. Among different redistributive policies, the education policy and fiscal policy (the taxation system in particular) are commonly used by central governments to reduce income disparity. Policies that do not aim at reducing inequality may also affect the distribution of income (see, for example, Vanhoudt 1996).

The taxation system is a key device to redistribute income. King (1980) discusses the redistributive effects and the benefits of taxes in the U.S., the U.K., and Sweden. Johnson and Webb (1993) indicate that there is a clear relationship between changes in the taxation system and changes in income inequality. Hayes and Slottje (1989) argue that states in the U.S. with more progressive sales and personal income taxes tend to have a higher degree of inequality. However, high aggregate local taxes progressivity can reduce inequality.

Education is another major vehicle to reduce income inequality. The human capital theory suggests that education is a major determinant of earnings which is an important factor affecting income inequality. O'Neil (1984) states that education has been instrumental in improving people's lives and economic status. Birdsall et al. (1995) argue that investment in education is a key to sustained growth and that it reduces income inequality. Tilak (1994) concludes that for education to contribute positively to income distribution, public subsidies must be judiciously distributed.

Although public housing policies are not commonly used in countries other than Hong Kong to narrow household income dispersion, government-subsidized housing blocks are widely available in Hong Kong and Singapore. As Hong Kong has a *laissez-faire* economy, government intervention is minimal. The housing policy is the main vehicle by which the government redistribute income. Half of Hong Kong's population lives in government-assisted rental units or in government built home-ownership flats. Previous studies, for example Wong and Liu (1988), argue that the public housing policy has failed to transfer income to the genuinely poor. In Chapter 4 of this book, I will assess whether the public housing programme can achieve its redistributive objective.

Economic Growth in the Post-War Period

The World Bank (1995) classifies Hong Kong as a high-income economy, defined as having a per capita income of US$48,626 or more in 1993. Hong Kong's gross national product (GNP) per capita for 1993 was US$19,700 (Census & Statistics Department 1996b). Explanations for the growth of Hong Kong and other Asian economies have long been at the top of development economists' research agenda (see, for example, Chen 1979, Oshima 1987, Lin and Tuan 1993). This section summarizes Hong Kong's economic growth in the post-war period.

In measuring the growth of an economy, we rely primarily on official gross domestic product (GDP) and GNP estimates. The

Table 2.1

The Ratio of GNP to GDP for Selected Economies

Economy	Ratio
Australia	0.967
Canada	0.966
France	0.992
Germany	0.996
Hong Kong	1.011
Japan	1.009
Singapore	1.014
Taiwan	1.016

Source: Census & Statistics Department, press release of 13 November 1995

Table 2.2

GDP by Component at Current Market Prices

Component	1961	1965	1970	1975	1980	1985	1990	1995
PCE#	5.6	8.6	14.9	31.7	84.7	167.5	330.5	653.7
GCE*	0.6	0.9	1.6	3.5	8.7	19.8	43.3	95.3
Investment+	1.8	4.9	4.7	11.4	49.7	58.7	159.5	387.7
Exports of goods	3.9	6.5	15.2	29.8	98.2	235.2	639.9	1,344.1
Imports of goods	6.0	9.0	17.6	33.5	111.8	232.6	645.2	1,495.7
Exports of services	2.4	3.2	6.5	11.8	29.2	61.1	142.3	291.0
Imports of services	0.9	1.3	2.4	5.5	17.0	37.9	87.7	164.7
GDP@ (HK$ billion)	7.4	13.9	23.0	49.3	141.8	271.7	582.5	1,111.4
Per capita (HK$'000)	2.3	3.9	5.8	11.2	28.0	49.8	102.1	179.6
GDP deflator ##	12.0	13.7	17.5	27.5	45.7	66.8	100.0	146.1

Source: Census & Statistics Deparment 1996a
Notes: All figures for GDP components are expressed in HK$ billion.
- # PCE is Private Consumption Expenditure
- * GCE is Government Consumption Expenditure
- + Investment = Gross domestic fixed capital formation + changes in inventories
- @ GDP = PCE + GCE + Investment + Exports - Imports
- ## GDP price deflator (1990=100)

Hong Kong government released the first GNP data series in 1995. Although some economic commentators predicted that the territory's GNP estimates would be much lower than its GDP estimates, based on the preliminary estimates, the ratio of Hong Kong's GNP to its GDP for 1993 was 1.011 (Census & Statistics Department 1996b). This ratio is comparable to that of other industrialized and newly developed economies. As is shown in Table 2.1, the ratios of GNP to GDP for selected economies were all close to one. The ratios for the four Asian economies in the table were very similar. The ratios of some industrialized economies, such as Canada and Germany, were less than one.

From Table 2.2, we can see that Hong Kong's GDP per capita at current market prices increased at an annual rate of 13.7% from 1961 to 1995. Taken at face value, this growth rate is truly remarkable. However, if the average inflation rate was higher than was the growth rate of GDP per capita, average real purchasing power actually decreased.

To assess whether Hong Kong's real income was decreasing or increasing during the period, we should study the changes in real GDP per capita. GDP estimates, measured at constant market prices, can be used to analyze the inflation problem in comparing data for different years. Moreover, per capita income data are adjusted for variations in population size. Thus, we can make use of per capita income data measured at constant market prices to assess the changes in the average purchasing power of an economy. In order to form a clear idea of the development of Hong Kong's economy, I depict in Figure 2.1 the growth pattern of Hong Kong's GDP per capita at constant (1990) market prices for the period 1961 to 1995. This figure clearly shows that Hong Kong's real GDP per capita increased fairly steadily during the period. After adjusting for changes in price level and population size, it became evident that the average purchasing power of Hong Kong people increased 6.3 times. In real term, Hong Kong's per capita income (measured at constant 1990 market prices) rose from HK$19,500 (US$2,500)

Figure 2.1
GDP per Capita at Constant (1990) Market Prices

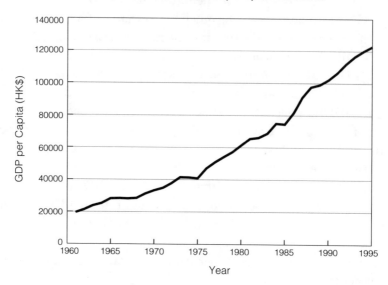

Source: Census & Statistics Department (1996a)

in 1961 to HK$122,900 (US$15,800) in 1995 (Census & Statistics Department 1996a).

Hong Kong's Economic Transformation

Until recently, the public was not particularly concerned about structural changes taking place in Hong Kong, because the labour market's employment level was almost at capacity, and the real wage was rising much faster than inflation. Hong Kong residents were enjoying the fruits of economic success. However, Suen (1995) argues that there were clear signs that Hong Kong was undergoing restructuring as early as the early 1970s. His analysis shows that the rate of economic transformation has accelerated since the 1980s. He also concludes that there is no evidence that structural change increases aggregate unemployment or underemployment in the

Table 2.3
Rates of Economic Transformation, Hong Kong

Period	Index of Sectoral Shifts	Standard Deviation of Employment Growth
1961–1971	7.5	0.47
1971–1981	8.1	0.56
1981–1991	15.8	0.60

Source: Suen (1995)

Table 2.4
Index of Sectoral Shifts for Selected Economies

Economies	1982–1986	1987–1992
Hong Kong	3.58	8.90
Japan	2.05	2.22
Korea	8.48	6.50
Singapore	5.98	3.27
U.S.	2.94	2.16

Source: Suen (1995)

declining sectors. Nonetheless, the observed wage dispersion has widened, which has led to a higher degree of wage inequality. In this section, I document the sectoral shifts that have occurred in Hong Kong since the 1970s.

Various indicators suggest that the rate of economic transformation in Hong Kong was picking up in the late 1980s. Table 2.3 shows two measures of sectoral shifts.[1] The index of sectoral shifts in the first column can be interpreted as the minimum proportion of workers who have to change sectors as a result of sectoral shifts (Suen 1995). The second column of Table 2.3 presents the standard deviation of the growth rates of employment across different sectors. Both pieces of information provide clear evidence that the pace of economic restructuring in Hong Kong accelerated in the late 1980s. However, by looking at these numbers we cannot infer that the rate of structural change in Hong Kong was fast or slow. In

Figure 2.2
Distribution of the Working Population by Sector

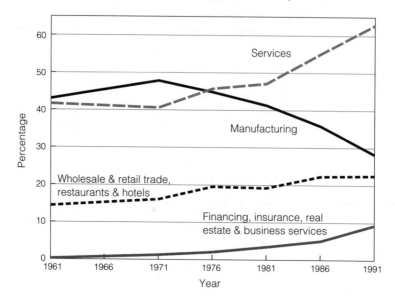

Source: Census & Statistics Department (1996a)

order to compare the rate of Hong Kong's economic transformation to that of other economies, I present an index of the sectoral
shift of Hong Kong, Japan, Korea, Singapore, and the U.S. in Table
2.4. From the table, we can see that in the period 1982 to 1986, the
rate of economic restructuring in Hong Kong was much slower than
was that of the other two Asian economies, Korea and Singapore.
As expected, the rate of structural change in developed countries
such as Japan and the U.S. was much slower. During the period
1987 to 1992, the pace of structural transformation in Hong Kong
picked up speed, and it surpassed that of other economies. This
explains why the public has been more concerned about structural
change in recent years.

The employment share of Hong Kong's manufacturing sector
started declining in the early 1970s. Figure 2.2 plots the changes in

percentage distribution of the working population in the manufacturing and service sectors of the economy. The figure clearly shows the changing sectoral composition of Hong Kong's economy. In 1971 manufacturing industries employed 47% of the domestic labour force. Since then, the employment share has declined gradually. It fell to 41% in 1981 and further decreased to 28% in 1991. As expected, the decline of the manufacturing sector came about in conjunction with the growing importance of the service sector. Today, the service sector employs more than 60% of the domestic workforce. From Figure 2.2, we can see that the lost employment share of the manufacturing sector was taken over by the service sector. The service sector includes four major industries, namely, (1) transport, storage, and communication; (2) wholesale and retail trade, restaurants, and hotels; (3) financing, insurance, real estate, and business services; and (4) community, social, and personal services. The service sector as a whole gained more than twenty percentage points in employment share in the period 1971 to 1991.[2]

Table 2.5 (next page) presents the working population by industry. The manufacturing sector employed about 512,000 workers in 1961 and that total employment rose to 990,000 in 1981. Between 1981 and 1991 the number dropped to 768,000. In ten years, the manufacturing sector lost 222,000 workers. Assuming that these workers all stayed in the labour market, the economy must have created an equal number of new jobs in other sectors to accommodate them. Creating more than 200,000 new jobs, not to mention matching workers (who were formerly employed in the manufacturing industry) with non-manufacturing vacancies would have been no easy task for any government. If these workers had not been sufficiently mobile, economists would have anticipated widespread unemployment due to a mismatch between skills and available opportunities. However, unemployment never exceeded 4% at any point during this period of abrupt change in sectoral composition. In fact, the unemployment rate declined to a record low level of 1.1% in 1989. In the same period, the service sector employed an additional 500,000 workers.

Chapter 2

Table 2.5
Working Population by Industry

Industry	1961	1971	1976	1981	1986	1991
Manufacturing	512	756	846	990	947	768
Construction	58	83	104	186	164	188
Wholesale & retail trade, restaurants & hotels	171	254	362	461	590	611
Transport, storage & communication	87	115	136	181	210	266
Finance, insurance, real estate & business services	19	41	62	116	170	287
Community, social & personal services	218	232	285	376	486	539
Others	126	102	73	93	76	56
Working Population	1,191	1,583	1,867	2,404	2,643	2,715

Sources: Census & Statistics Department, *Population Census Report*, various issues.
Note: All figures are expressed in thousands.

Among the four major services industries, (1) wholesale and retail trade, restaurants, and hotels, and (2) financing, insurance, real estate, and business services accounted for most of the increase in employment share. The other two groups experienced a smaller increase in employment share. In Figure 2.2, I also plot the changes in distribution of those employed in these two services industries. In the early 1960s the financing, insurance, real estate, and business service industries employed less than 2% of the working population. When trade between the East and the West started to pick up, Hong Kong acted as the bridge. Many multinational corporations chose Hong Kong as their regional headquarters. Almost all leading banks in the world have branches of one form or another in Hong Kong. By the 1980s Hong Kong had established itself as one of the world's leading financial centres. The adoption of the open-door policy by the People's Republic of China's government in the late 1970s fueled the growth of financing, insurance, real estate, and business services. This industry's prospects for the future hinge on the development of China's economy.

To support its increasing number of activities, the size of the financing, insurance, real estate, and business services industry expanded rapidly. A significant portion of the working population was absorbed into this industry, and its employment share rose from 1.6% in 1961 to 10.6% in 1991. In other words, the employment share of the industry increased by nine percentage points in thirty years. Moreover, the industry demands well-trained and educated workers. Workers previously employed in the manufacturing sector were less likely to be able to satisfy the requirements of the financing, insurance, real estate, and business services industry. Fortunately, the implementation of free and universal education provided timely inputs into the industry. The educational level of an average worker in the labour market today is much higher than it ever was before. However, the industry is changing rapidly, and its investment instruments are becoming more and more complicated. To sustain its growth, a steady inflow of qualified employees is vital. The recent expansion of tertiary education in the territory has helped meeting the demand. In addition, Hong Kong workers are constantly upgrading themselves either through on-the-job training or through part-time study. Numerous sub-degree, degree, and post-graduate courses are offered in the territory. All this has contributed to smoothen Hong Kong's transition from a manufacturing economy to a service economy. One negative aspect of this rapid development, however, has been the escalating cost of renting prime office space. Offices in Hong Kong are among the most expensive in the world to rent, and this will decrease the territory's attractiveness to foreign investors.

The economic development of China has the potential to influence Hong Kong's status as an international financial centre. Moreover, some cities in China want to replace Hong Kong as an international trade centre. However, it is very unlikely that any of these cities will be able to fill Hong Kong's shoes at any time in the near future. At the very least, they must equip themselves before they can directly compete with Hong Kong. As a large and

Table 2.6
Sectoral Shifts and Change in Earnings Variance

Change in Variance	1976–1991	1986–1991
Due to composition change	0.058	0.013
Between-Industry	0.020	0.001
Within-Industry	0.038	0.012
Due to change in variance	0.026	0.032
Between-Industry	–0.028	–0.008
Within-Industry	0.054	0.040
Total Change	0.083	0.046

Source: Suen (1995)

economically powerful country, China could easily develop a port to rival Hong Kong's. It could also invest heavily in building a particular city's infrastructure. But Hong Kong's most valuable asset is a large pool of diligent, industrious, flexible, and capable people. In addition, a sizable portion of Hong Kong's workforce is bilingual and can communicate with both Chinese and Westerners. Hong Kong people understand the cultures of both worlds and have established good working relationships with the territory's trading partners. Although Hong Kong's position as an international financial and trade centre will not be jeopardized by neighbouring cities soon, the gap between the territory and its competitors is narrowing. Moreover, competition in international financial markets is very keen, and it is necessary to constantly monitor the latest market developments. At the same time, Hong Kong must invest in human capital and train the next generation.

If the financing, insurance, real estate, and business services industry did not absorb workers from the shrinking manufacturing sector, where did these surplus workers go? There are several possibilities. Some workers previously engaged in manufacturing industries found it difficult to secure new jobs. They either remained unemployed for a prolonged period or decided to leave the labour market and go elsewhere. Poorly educated workers with limited experience outside manufacturing were particularly hard hit. It is believed that workers in the textile and apparel industries, as well as in the plastics and rubber products industries, suffered the most. Other workers tried to equip themselves for new jobs through retraining. Some ex-factory workers joined the wholesale and retail trade, or began working in restaurants and hotels. Most of them took low-level positions, such as janitors in hotels, that required little formal education. In many cases, they earned considerably less than they did in their manufacturing sector jobs. There is a general belief that large-scale sectoral shifts will lead to substantial changes in relative earnings. In the next section, I discuss the possible relationship between sectoral shifts and income inequality.

Sectoral Shifts and Income Inequality in Hong Kong

In the economic literature, there are numerous examples of researchers trying to establish the relationship between economic transformation and income distribution. For the case of Hong Kong, Suen (1995) attempts to analyze the effects of sectoral shifts on income inequality by decomposing the change in an indicator of income inequality called "variance of log earnings" for the period 1976 to 1991. His results are summarized in Table 2.6. Based on the four census files (which are the same as those used in this book) made available by the government, he discovers that change in industrial composition does matter in explaining rising income inequality. Since industry classification for the economically active population changed during the four census years, Suen reclassifies for the purpose of comparison all industries into twenty-five broad categories across different years.

Looking at the first column in Table 2.6, we can see that the variance in log earnings increased by 0.083 in the period 1976 to 1991. Changes in industrial composition alone explain 70% (or 0.058) of that increase in variance. In other words, if the distribution of the working population within the twenty-five industries remained unchanged during this period, the degree of inequality in log earnings could have decreased by 70%. Thus, sectoral shifts account for the bulk of the increase in income dispersion in the period. However, if we focus on more recent years, we see a different picture. For the period 1986 to 1991, the "within-industry" increase is the most important factor in explaining the overall rise in inequality. Moreover, changes in sectoral shares, i.e., changes in distribution of the working population within the twenty-five industries, only account for 28% of the overall increase in variance. In short, economic restructuring is the major factor responsible for the overall rise in income inequality in Hong Kong in the period 1976 to 1991. However, in more recent years, sectoral shifts, i.e. inequality of wages "between" industries, are not an important factor in explaining the rising income dispersion.

Hong Kong in Perspective

It is well known that Hong Kong's economy has grown rapidly in the last few decades. During the course of this growth, the economy has undergone significant restructuring. The shrinking of the manufacturing sector is associated with the expansion of the service sector. Although the labour market adjusted smoothly to changes in the sectoral composition of the economy, there has been an increase in the level of income disparity. Since the seminal work of Kuznets (1955) on economic growth and income inequality appeared, the issue has remained a topic of active research. In the literature, there is little consensus on whether inequality affects growth, or vice versa. Moreover, the relationship between sectoral shifts and income inequality has yet to be established by empirical evidence.

In the next chapter, I take a closer look at income distribution in Hong Kong. As they are in the literature, various socioeconomic variables such as gender and immigration are used to analyze the income inequality situation in Hong Kong. Previous studies indicate that public policies that aim at reducing income disparity may not achieve their desired objectives. Chapter 4 of this book addresses the effects of public policies, with particular emphasis on the education policy and the public housing policy, on income distribution in Hong Kong.

Notes

1. See Suen (1995) for further discussion on and a calculation of the index of sectoral shifts.

2. Up to December 1990 figures were analyzed by the international standard of industries classfication (ISIC). As of March 1991 the Hong Kong standard of classification (HSIC) took the place of the ISIC for the statistical classification of activities in Hong Kong. Figures from March 1991 onwards are therefore available only in the HSIC and are not strictly comparable to those from the past series, which are in the ISIC.

CHAPTER 3

Income Distribution
in Hong Kong

In this chapter, I document the stylized facts of the income distribution of Hong Kong's working population. The measures of income inequality employed in this chapter include the Gini coefficient, the Lorenz curve, the coefficient of variation, the variance of the logarithmic income, and a set of quantile ratios. As the Gini coefficient is frequently used and misused by the public, I explain its derivation in detail. I also offer some precautions against using the Gini coefficient to measure changes in income inequality.

In the second section of this chapter, I describe the data set used in this study. Since gender always makes a difference in income-related issues, I subdivide the data set into male and female sub-samples. I analyze the income distribution of both the working population and of households in Hong Kong. As readers may wish to know more about people of Chinese ethnicity, I take a closer look at a sub-sample of the data set which includes those born in China or Hong Kong. The empirical results in this book suggest that incomes in Hong Kong have become more disparate in recent years than they were in the past. This is true for both the distribution of personal main-employment income and for the distribution of household income. I show that income distribution is more disparate among Hong Kong natives than among the immigrants from China.

Measures of Income Inequality

Many commentators and researchers use the Gini coefficient as the only measure of the inequality of income distribution. They compare Gini coefficients of different economies or of different periods in a particular economy. However, the Gini coefficient is just one of the many measurements of income inequality. Basically, it is a "scalar measure"; that is, all the features of inequality are compressed into a single index or number.

It is easy to understand why people prefer a scalar measure to a multi-dimensional tool, especially when they want to indicate the direction in which income inequality is changing. A multi-dimensional measure makes the job of directly comparing different economies or different periods in a given economy very difficult. For example, suppose that we are interested in two income-related attributes, A and B, of a population. While attribute A recorded a higher degree inequality from period 1 to period 2, attribute B moved toward a higher degree of equality. Under these circumstances, we cannot say that period 2 is less equal than period 1, or vice versa. Even in a hypothetical two-attributes, two-period case, not to mention in the real, complex, and heterogeneous world, we cannot come to a decisive conclusion about the change in income inequality. Thus, researchers try to compress all the attributes of inequality into a single (scalar) measure. Unfortunately, the Gini coefficient and some other frequently used measurements of unequal income distribution are sometimes abused by commentators or researchers. In this section, I present other standard measurements of income inequality. The concept of "income inequality" is also discussed.

What is Income Inequality?

Although the term "income inequality" appears frequently in newspapers and magazines, it has no commonly agreed-upon meaning. When someone talks about the inequality of income distribution for a particular population, we have to know what he or she means by "income". We also have to determine whether he or she is referring to income inequality for individuals or for households. In the narrowest sense, income is regarded as payment for work. Some people view income as also including returns on investments. Economists, however, use a more comprehensive concept of income and define it as the increase in a person's command over resources during a given time period. In this book, both concepts of income are used. In order to minimize any ambiguity, I define "unadjusted" and "adjusted" income as follows:

1. Unadjusted Income: Money received over a calendar month, especially as payment for work or as interest on investments.
2. Adjusted Income: A person's or family's total command over resources during a calendar month, including both earnings and unearned income, the latter of which includes dividends or interest received on investments and transfer payments received from the government in the form of subsidized public housing, welfare payments, old age and (or) disability benefits, and the like.

Adjusted income also covers employee benefits, including payments in kind and deferred payment. Hong Kong workers enjoy variable lengths of paid leave under different categories such as casual leave, vacation leave, long leave, maternity leave, and sick leave. When workers take leaves, they receive days off instead of cash. We call these non-monetary benefits payments in kind. Other examples of payments in kind to employees are the provision of medical insurance, staff quarters, and company vehicles. Workers may also receive "deferred" payments for their work. Year-end bonuses, retirement benefits, and contract-end gratuities are all part of the compensation a worker receives for his or her work. Technically speaking, the sum of employment earnings, payments in kind, and deferred payment is known as "employee compensation". Adjusted income should also include transfer payments received from the government. I have to stress that I am *not* arguing that adjusted income is preferable to unadjusted income. Rather, I simply wish to clarify the meaning of the term "income" in relation to inequality in income distribution. Different concepts of income can serve different purposes. It is very difficult, if not impossible, to find an all-purpose candidate that satisfies all the requirements of heterogeneous researchers.

Most research studies report measures of inequality in unadjusted income. This is understandable, as unadjusted personal income data are readily available in official statistical publications. Moreover, the interpretation of these income inequality measures is rather straightforward. On the other hand, the derivation of adjusted income measures depends on the individual researcher's preference, which is somewhat arbitrary. Using the same set of data, researchers may come up with conflicting results. This greatly limits the transportability and comparability of adjusted measure of income distribution. Cowell (1995) points out that two key characteristics of an income index are: (1) it should be measurable and (2) it should be comparable among different persons.[1] These two attributes of an income index are in favour of using the unadjusted income concept. Following in the footsteps of most researchers, I mainly deal with the concept of unadjusted income in the rest of this book, and the adjective "unadjusted" is dropped for simplicity. Whenever I refer to adjusted income, I will spell it out explicitly in order to avoid confusion.

In his dissertation in urban planning, Wu (1973) attempts to adjust the income distribution of households. He adds a government "subsidy" to a household income to derive an adjusted "total income" of households living in government-aided housing. Surprisingly, Wu's calculations lead to a greater degree of inequality in income distribution. The official Gini coefficient estimate for 1971 stood at 0.43. Wu, however, argues that the Gini coefficient using adjusted household income should be 0.74. If Wu's argument were correct, it would mean that the government would be unable to achieve the redistributive objective of its public housing policy. Chow and Papanek (1981) point out that Wu incorrectly adjusted the Gini coefficient upward instead of downward. They believe that the estimate should be close to the official Gini coefficient, even taking into account subsidized public housing.

Concepts of Income Inequality Measure

There are quite a number of income inequality measures used by different researchers. It is useful to have some criteria by which to assess which income inequality measures are more desirable than others. In general, economists agree that an income inequality measure should possess certain properties. These are:

1. Income scale independence — a measure should be robust to the chosen income scale. For example, the reported measures should be the same whether the data is expressed in Hong Kong dollars or in pounds sterling. The mean and the variance of income data will change when we change the unit of measurement, but an income inequality measure should not be changed. Most commonly used indices satisfy this condition, but income inequality measures such as Dalton's inequality indices vary when everyone's income changes by the same proportion.

2. Population size independence — a measure should not depend on the size of the population of a given economy. Suppose a researcher measures the inequality of n persons in a given economy. When we merge another group of n persons, which have the same level of measured inequality, into that economy, the resulting income inequality measure should remain the same. In other words, the income inequality measure of the combined economy of 2n persons is the same as is the income inequality measure of the economy of n persons. However, Cowell (1995) casts doubts as to whether the principle of population size independence is really desirable.

3. Pigou-Dalton condition — a measure should increase when we transfer a positive amount of income from a poorer person to a richer person.

4. Decomposability — this condition implies that there should be a coherent relationship between inequality in the whole population and inequality in its sub-groups (Cowell 1995). Analytically, this property is useful for researchers who wish to study the underlying causes of changes in inequality of income distribution.

Not all commonly used income inequality measures possess all the above-mentioned properties. For example, the widely used Gini coefficient satisfies the first three conditions, but it cannot be decomposed (condition four).[2] Condition four is particularly useful in the analysis of the effects of variations in between-group and within-group inequalities if the composition of a given population has changed. Although Cowell (1995) carefully explains that variance of logarithmic income doesn't meet the strict conditions necessary for unambiguous decomposability, Lam (1995) selects the variance of logarithmic income as her income inequality measure. She decomposes the variance of logarithmic earnings into within-group and between-group variances. She concludes that the increase in income inequality in Hong Kong over the period 1981 to 1991 is mainly due to the increase in within-group inequality. In this book, I also decompose the variance of logarithmic income, even though it is not decomposable in the strict sense.

Conceptual Problems of Inequality Measures

When people talk about inequality in income distribution, they often focus on the condition of those on the bottom rungs of the economic ladder. It is important, however, to distinguish between poverty and income inequality. When we discuss poverty, we usually focus on a very small segment of the population with income levels below some specified "poverty line" (Cowell 1995), poverty line referring to the minimum subsistence income level in a given economy. On the other hand, the income inequality issue is usually used in reference to the whole society. It is possible for poverty to lessen while inequality in income distribution is increasing. This book deals with the latter but not the former issue.

Whenever there is increased income inequality, there are voices urging the government to implement a redistributive policy. In considering the merits of such a policy, we must ask ourselves whether perfect equality in income distribution is really desirable. I would argue that, on the contrary, it is highly undesirable. As an example, let us suppose that there are only two workers, worker A and worker B, in an economy. Worker A is extremely hard working and productive, while worker B is rather lazy and unproductive. Isn't it unfair to distribute output (income) equally between them? Shouldn't income reflect an individual's contribution to society? However, an equitable society is not one in which output is shared equally among members irrespective of their individual performance. As long as workers A and B have equal access to education and work opportunities, most people would agree that a certain degree of income inequality is acceptable and equitable. Thus, when we study the income inequality issue, we have to distinguish between the equality of opportunity and the equality of results. Moreover, we must take into consideration the relationship between equity and income equality.

A society is not a static entity. The composition of a dynamic city like Hong Kong may change drastically within as little as ten years time. Households classified as poor a decade ago may be wealthy now. Inequality in income distribution in a society with a high degree of social mobility may be a strong impetus for hard work. People living in a community with a high degree of income equality lack the motivation to strive for success. As Becker (1995) says, increased income inequality may be an engine that drives an economy toward more rapid economic growth.

Lastly, most applications of income inequality analysis concentrate on income distribution at a point in time. Very often, researchers pay no attention to the variation in income over a person's lifetime. Suppose, for example, that all workers in a given society have equal earning ability and the same working life span. In this society, the only source of variation in income is the amount of work experience individual workers possess. If we study lifetime income distribution in the society, we will observe perfect income equality. However, workers are at different stages of their lives. An analysis at a point in time will inevitably show a fair degree of income inequality. New employees receive lower wages simply because they lack experience. Any public policy that directs more subsidies to this low-income group is unjust. All the above-mentioned conceptual problems with income inequality measures boil down to the fact that there are many dimensions to be considered when analyzing income distribution. It is dangerous and misleading to rely on a single inequality measure upon which to make policy pleas.

What is the Gini Coefficient?

There are many income inequality measures in the literature, and they can be broadly classified as scalar inequality indices and multi-dimensional inequality indices. Scalar inequality indices are those such as the Gini coefficient, the coefficient of variation, the variance, the range, the quantile ratio, the variance of logarithms, relative mean deviation, Atkinson's index, and Theil's entropy index. As far as multi-dimensional inequality measures are concerned, most discussions in the literature are academic and theoretical in nature. There is no consensus as to which multi-dimensional inequality index should be adopted. For example, Tsui (1992) develops a multi-dimensional mathematical model to analyze inequality in income distribution. In addition to these income inequality indices, graphical methods, especially the Lorenz curve, are used frequently. Although the Lorenz curve can be used to derive the relative mean deviation, it is normally associated with the Gini coefficient.

In this book, I mainly use three income inequality measures, namely, the Gini coefficient, the variance of logarithms, and the quantile ratio. I also employ the human-capital approach in estimating returns to education in the following chapter when I discuss the relationship between the government's education policy and income distribution. Graphical presentations, of the Lorenz curve in particular, are used judiciously to illustrate the text.

Many readers have heard of the Gini coefficient, but they may not know exactly what it is. Thus, I explain the derivation of Gini coefficient in more detail below.

There are a variety of ways to define the Gini co- efficient. One definition states that the coefficient is the average difference between all possible pairs of incomes in the population expressed as a proportion of total income (Cowell 1995).[3] This verbal definition and the formal mathematical definition in the chapter endnote may confuse readers. A Lorenz curve can help to explain the concept more clearly.

Suppose there are n persons with income in a population. First, we arrange them in ascending order of income and calculate the accumulated income share for each observation. Then we plot them in Figure 3.1, with the cumulative population share as the x-axis and the cumulative income share as the y-axis. The resulting graph is called a Lorenz curve. If the total income of a given population is shared equally among all n persons, the cumulative income share of each observation *should* equal the cumulative population share. That is to say, if perfect equality exists in a given population, each person should get $1/n$ of the total income. In this case, the Lorenz curve will lie on the diagonal of Figure 3.1. A hypothetical Lorenz curve is plotted in Figure 3.1. The area between the Lorenz curve and the diagonal is Area A, and the area below the Lorenz curve is Area B. If total income is shared equally among all persons, the size of Area A is zero. The higher the degree of inequality in distribution of income, the larger the area of A. With the aid of Figure 3.1, we can now define the Gini coefficient as:

Gini Coefficient = Area A / (Area A + Area B).

This equation shows that the Gini coefficient lies between 0 and 1. The higher the coefficient, the higher the degree of income inequality. Under perfect equality, the Gini coefficient equals zero. Under another extreme condition, if one person earns all the income in a society and the rest earn nothing, the Gini coefficient equals one.

Figure 3.1
A Hypothetical Lorenz Curve

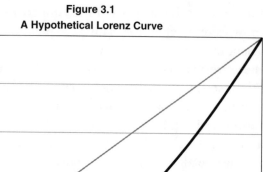

Figure 3.2
Intersecting Lorenz Curves

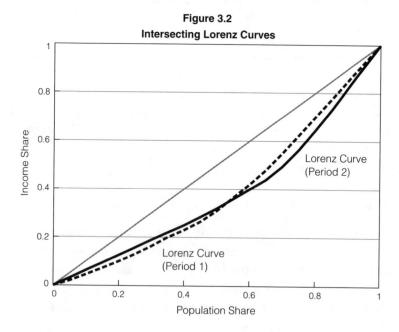

Interpreting a Lorenz curve and a Gini coefficient is very straightforward. However, comparing two Lorenz curves or two Gini coefficients is a nontrivial task. When a Lorenz curve lies completely below another Lorenz curve, we can say with certainty that the lower curve reflects higher income inequality. The corresponding Gini coefficients tell the same story — that the one with a higher value represents higher income inequality. But when two Lorenz curves intersect, it is not clear which one indicates a higher level of income inequality. It is also misleading to compare the corresponding Gini coefficients of two intersecting Lorenz curves.

To illustrate the last point, see the two hypothetical Lorenz curves in Figure 3.2. Suppose the dotted line in the figure refers to the income distribution of a given population in period one, and the solid line refers to the income distribution in period two of the same population. The Gini coefficient for period one is slightly lower than is that for period two. From the figure, we can see that the first 55% of the population earn a lower share of total income in period one than they do in period two. The two Lorenz curves intersect when the population share reaches 0.55. After the intersection point, the top 45% of the population in period one receives a higher income share than it does in period two. Under these conditions, we cannot conclude that income inequality has either increased or decreased between period one and period two. If we compare the two Gini coefficients, we may jump to the conclusion that income inequality increased between period one and period two. However, if we study the figure carefully and pay close attention to the income share of the bottom half of the population, we may find that there is a greater degree of income equality in period two than there is in period one. This is because in period two, the bottom half of the population gets a larger share of the pie. (As was previously mentioned, when people talk about inequality in income distribution, they are usually particularly concerned with the situation of the those whose income levels lie in the bottom 20% to 30% of the population. Almost all government redistribution policies cater to that group. From a social point of view, people generally prefer the bottom group to receive an increased share of total income, other things being equal.) This example illustrates one important point that should be considered when interpreting the Gini coefficient. When studying income distribution, it is advisable to consider other factors besides the absolute difference in Gini coefficient estimates.

Description of the Data Set

The main data sources used in this book are the 1% random sub-samples of the 1976, 1981, 1986, and 1991 population census files. I also extract useful information from official statistical publications and various departmental annual reports. This book looks at the income distribution of individuals as well as house-holds. For the income distribution of individuals, I focus on the working population. It would be better if we could select those who are full-time workers. Unfortunately, the 1991 population census does not collect information on work hours. To make the data across different census years comparable, I have had to select the working population as a whole, including both part-time and full-time workers. Fortunately, the underemployment rates in these years were very low by international standards. Moreover, Lui and Suen (1993) show that the size of the coefficient of the hours of work variable on log earnings is small (0.0015, 0.0011 and 0.0003 for 1976, 1981 and 1986 respectively). Thus, from the 1% census samples, I have selected the following:
  (1) those aged between 15 and 64;
  (2) those who were working in the census reference week;
  (3) those who received positive earnings from main employment; and
  (4) those who were not full-time students or unpaid family workers.

The term income is narrowly defined when studying the income distribution of individuals. Basically, I look at the distribution of main employment earnings instead of at total income. In the data set, the top code for income was 99,998, which refers to monthly income in the amount of HK$99,998 or more. In all four census years, only a very small percentage of records had incomes in this range. For simplicity's sake, I make no attempt to impute the real income. As a result, the income inequality measures reported in this book are slightly lower than the actual value, but the difference should not be significant.

On the other hand, when I discuss the distribution of household income, the term income covers the employment earnings and other income of all household members. In analyzing the income distribution of households, the sample selection criteria is much simpler. I include all households in the census files in my analysis. As Hong Kong is predominantly a Chinese society, readers maybe wish to know more about the distribution of income of those born in Hong Kong and in China. For this reason, I also perform data analysis on a sub-sample of Hong Kong natives and Chinese immigrants. Before I present the results of my analysis, I want to emphasize that the composition of Hong Kong's population changed drastically between 1976 and 1991. Any changes in income distribution are due to a combination of forces. Structural change, economic growth, and composition change all play a part in explaining the resulted variation in income inequality.

Income Distribution of the Working Population

Table 3.1 summarizes the socioeconomic characteristics of the population during the four census years. I have calculated the figures in the tables from the 1% random sub-sample of the census files, and they may deviate slightly from official figures. The mean age of the labour force increased from 34.4 in 1976 to 35.5 in 1991. As the mean age increased, one may expect that the average amount of work experience also increased. In this book, I compute the years of work experience as follows:

Working Experience = Age − Years of schooling − 6.

Contrary to general expectation, however, the average amount of work experience declined by 2.5 years between 1976 and 1991.

Table 3.1

Socioeconomic Characteristics of the Working Population

Characteristics (Variables)	1976	1981	1986	1991
Age	34.4	33.8	34.7	35.5
Years of schooling	7.2	7.7	8.7	9.3
Years of working experience	21.3	20.1	20.0	18.8
Main employment income ($)	982	1,999	3,642	7,754
Gender (%)				
Male	68.5	66.2	63.8	62.5
Female	31.5	33.8	36.2	37.5
Marital status (%)				
Single	43.0	43.4	40.2	37.5
Married	54.3	54.0	56.8	60.0
Separated / Widowed	2.7	2.7	2.9	2.5
Place of birth (%)				
Hong Kong	43.2	48.0	54.8	58.3
China (including Macau)	53.6	46.7	41.0	35.1
Others	3.2	5.3	4.2	6.6

Notes: Calculations are based on 1% census files.

This information may seem puzzling. However, if we look at the years-of-schooling variable, it is easily understood. On average, a worker received 9.3 years of schooling in 1991, which is 2.1 more years of schooling than the average worker received in 1976. The free and compulsory education policy adopted by the Hong Kong government in the 1970s has had an impact on the labour market. As it turns out, the government's decision to implement this policy was a prudent one. The growing importance of services suggest a general upgrading in labour demand. If the workforce had not been upgraded during this period, it could not have sustained the rapid economic transformation. In terms of main employment income, the workforce as a whole reaped the benefits of economic success. In 1976 an average worker received HK$982 per month. This amount would have been HK$7,754 in 1991 at current market prices. In real terms, main employment income increased at an annual rate of 5.2% between 1976 and 1991. During this period, the per capita GDP at constant (1990) prices increased 2.3 times, representing an annual growth rate of 5.6%. Apparently, the income level of Hong Kong's labour force rose at the same rate at which the economy as a whole was growing.

From Table 3.1, we can see that female workers constituted about one-third of the Hong Kong workforce in 1976 and that this ratio increased slightly to 37.5% in 1991. With better educational opportunities in the 1970s, more females chose to enter the labour market after completing their formal education. As a result, the participation rate of females in the workforce increased a fair amount, peaking at 51.2% in 1986 (Census & Statistics Department 1978, 1993). Lui and Suen (1993) argue that the increase in the rate of female participation in the labour force is one of the main driving forces behind the reduction in the gender earnings gap in the period 1976 to 1986.

Prior to 1974 the Hong Kong government admitted all immigrants from China into the territory. Since then, the government has implemented a more restrictive immigration policy. When it abolished the "reach base" policy on 23 October 1980, the inflow of Chinese immigrants was brought under the control of both the Chinese and the Hong Kong governments.[4] In light of this information, it is not surprising that Chinese immigrants constituted more than half of the working population in 1976. The tightened immigration policy impacted the composition of the workforce in later years. By 1991 immigrants from China made up about one-third of the workforce.

In considering the income distribution of the working population, we also need to take into account the contributions foreign workers have made to Hong Kong's economy. In 1976 workers born outside Hong Kong or China made up only of 3.2% of the working population. This percentage increased to 6.6 in 1991. In terms of absolute numbers, there were about 60,000 foreign workers in the Hong Kong labour market in 1976 and 180,000 in 1991. A significant portion of these foreign workers were domestic helpers from the Philippines and other Asian countries. Suen (1994) shows that the presence of a domestic helper in a home raises the conditional probability of female labour force participation. However, he suggests that the increased use of domestic helpers does not

Table 3.2
Measures of Income Inequality of the Working Population

Inequality Indicators	1976	1981	1986	1991
Gini coefficient	0.377	0.384	0.406	0.421
Coefficient of variation	1.311	1.424	1.274	1.204
Log income				
Mean	6.639	7.344	7.917	8.657
Variance	0.398	0.406	0.457	0.484
Quantile ratio				
P_{90}/P_{75}	1.500	1.625	1.538	1.625
P_{90}/P_{50}	2.143	2.167	2.308	2.364
P_{90}/P_{10}	3.750	4.063	4.425	4.643
P_{70}/P_{25}	2.000	1.942	2.053	2.000
P_{50}/P_{25}	1.400	1.456	1.368	1.375
P_{50}/P_{10}	1.750	1.875	1.917	1.964

Note: Calculations are based on 1% census files.

have a noticeable effect on the rate of female participation in the labour force. Nevertheless, he argues that the use of domestic helpers can bring about substantial gains to the families concerned.

From Table 3.1, we can see that the average main employment income of the working population increased substantially during the period in question. However, the table reveals nothing about income distribution. Did the income of the bottom 20% of the population rise faster than did that of the top 20%? Did income inequality increase over the period 1976 to 1991? To answer these questions, I present some common measures of income inequality of the working population in Table 3.2. In addition to using the Gini coefficient, I also tabulate three sets of income inequality measures, namely, the coefficient of variation, the quantile ratio, and the variance of logarithmic income. Basically, these three sets of income inequality indices are used to measure the relative dispersion of main employment income. Not all of them possess all four desirable properties discussed on page 35. However, all of them are independent of the income scale.

Before analyzing the results, it will be useful to briefly describe what these indices are. First, the coefficient of variation is simply the standard deviation of income divided by mean income:

Coefficient of Variation = Standard Deviation / Mean.

Standard deviation is a measure of dispersion, but it is not income scale independent. The coefficient of variation is used to standardize the standard deviation such that the resulting index is income scale independent. The higher the coefficient, the higher the level of income dispersion and the higher the level of income inequality. The next index, the variance of logarithmic income, is quite similar to the coefficient of variation. We begin by taking the (natural) logarithm of raw income and then compute the variance. The higher the variance of logarithmic income, the higher the level of income inequality.

If we arrange the working population in ascending order of main employment income, the 90th percentile, denoted as P_{90} in this book, refers to the income level which is above that of 90% of the workforce and below that of the top 10% of the same workforce. The quantile ratio is the ratio of two relevant quantiles. For example, P_{75}/P_{25} refers to the income level at the 75th percentile divided by the income level at the 25th percentile of distribution of main employment income. The higher the ratio, the higher the level of income dispersion. Six commonly used quantile ratios are presented in Table 3.2. If an economy is moving towards increased equality, all the indices will lower over the years. On the other hand, if the economy is moving towards increased income inequality, these indices will increase.

Reading across the first row of Table 3.2, we can see that the Gini coefficient increased steadily throughout the report period. The Gini coefficient of income distribution stood at 0.377 in 1976, and it had risen by 0.007 by 1981. By 1986 the coefficient had risen by 0.406, and it had risen by 0.421 by 1991. In fifteen years, the Gini coefficient increased by 0.044, which suggests that income distribution in Hong Kong became more uneven during this period. However, as explained from page 36 to 38, when considering

Figure 3.3
Lorenz Curves for 1976 and 1991

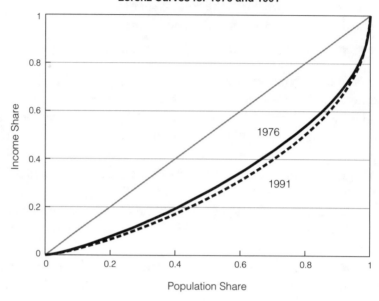

income distribution we should not only compare the difference in values of the Gini coefficient but should also consider other factors. In order to conclude that income inequality in 1991 was greater than it was in 1976, we have to prove that the Lorenz curve for 1991 lies entirely below that for 1976. To analyze the changes in income distribution, I plot the Lorenz curves for 1976 and 1991 in Figure 3.3. I could have depicted four Lorenz curves in the same figure, but these curves cluster together, making it difficult to distinguish between them.

In Figure 3.3, the dotted line corresponds to the Lorenz curve for 1991, and the solid line represents that for 1976. Although these two curves are very close to each other, the dotted line lies completely below the solid line. This corresponds to the fact that the Gini coefficient for 1991 is higher than is that for 1976. These two pieces of information suggest that income distribution in Hong Kong was more unequal in 1991 than it was in 1976. While the Hong Kong economy was growing increasingly prosperous, its labour market was moving towards a higher rate of inequality in income distribution.

In recent years, elected members of the Legislative Council have put forward numerous motions urging the government to increase its expenditure on social welfare. They have argued that the lower class is suffering despite the fact that the economy has been experiencing continuous positive real growth. Some of them have asserted that the rising degree of inequality is due to rapid economic transformation.

The results arrived at in this book suggest that their first argument is quite reasonable. However, the evidence gathered here does not prove that economic restructuring is the main cause of increased income inequality. As a matter of fact, increased wage inequality has also been observed in other developed countries (see, for example, Green et al. 1992, Katz and Ravenga 1992). If we want to argue that sectoral shifts in Hong Kong have led to increased income inequality, we have to make sure that the composition of the lowest economic group has remained identical throughout the period. If its composition has changed, rising income dispersion may in fact be due to its changing composition and not to economic transformation. The non-comparability of income recipients over time makes a direct comparison of measures of income inequality impractical. What I am suggesting here is that while economic restructuring in Hong Kong is one possible reason for increased inequality in income distribution, such a causal relationship cannot be established lightly. To establish such a causal relationship, as Suen (1995) also points out, we have to make use of a longitudinal data set to show that the worst-off group of workers are made even worse off over time.

In addition to employing the Gini coefficient, economists often use a variance of the logarithm of income as an indicator of income inequality. Looking at the last row of Table 3.2, the changes in the variance of log income tell the same story as does the Gini coefficient. The variance was at its lowest in 1976, and it rose slightly to 0.406 in 1981. The variance of log income increased to 0.457 in 1986, and it increased further to 0.421 in 1991. Comparing the variance of log income in 1991 with that of 1976, one can see that income dispersion widened by a large margin over the period.

Another inequality indicator, the coefficient of variation, tells a different story from that told by the variance in log income and by the Gini coefficient. According to the inequality indicator, overall income dispersion decreased from 1976 to 1991. This result contrasts sharply with that suggested by the change in the Gini coefficient. The strange behaviour of the coefficient of variation is due to the fact that the mean rose faster than the standard deviation did during the period. The seemingly conflicting results bring up an important issue to consider when choosing appropriate income inequality measures with which to analyze the distribution of income. Hamermesh and Rees (1993) point out that in the majority of cases a change in one part of income distribution will cause most measures of income inequality to move in the same direction. However, such a change could imply an increase or a decrease in inequality, depending on the income inequality measures used. Thus, it is advisable to use more than one inequality measure when analyzing the distribution of income. Hamermesh and Rees stress that no measure of inequality is necessarily correct for all purposes. Cowell (1995) presents a situation in which the variance of log income cannot satisfy the Pigou-Dalton condition (see the appendix to Cowell's text for details). In the present case, results presented in Table 3.2 indicate that income inequality increased between 1976 and 1991.

If we look at the quantile ratios presented in Table 3.2, we can gain a better understanding of the impact of changes on the income dispersion of different income groups. The first two ratios, P_{90}/P_{75} and P_{90}/P_{50}, recorded an increase in 1991 as compared with 1976. This suggests that the incomes of top earners, especially of the upper 25%, increased relative to the incomes of those who earned less, and that the income gap between higher- and lower-income groups widened. On the other hand, the third quantile ratio, P_{75}/P_{25}, remained the same during the period. The last two quantile ratios, however, clearly increased. This set of quantile ratios, as a whole, indicates that the increase in income inequality took place at the ends of the distribution rather than near the middle. This conjecture is confirmed by the large increase in the quantile ratio P_{90}/P_{10}. In the following sub-section, I further analyze this situation by dividing the sample into male and female sub-groups. The results show that overall income distribution for both male and female workers was becoming increasingly disparate.

Income Distribution by Gender

Discrimination based on gender in labour markets has long been a subject of active research among economists (see, for example, Blau and Kahn 1992) and sociologists (e.g., Rosenfeld and Kalleberg 1990) alike. However, income distribution by gender has received much less attention. In this section, I present stylized facts about income distribution by gender in Hong Kong. If we look at the socioeconomic characteristics of male and female workers in the labour market, we can observe clear differences between the two groups. On average, male workers were three to five years older than were their female counterparts in all four census years presented in Table 3.3. Due to their ages, the men naturally had more work experience. Although the gender earnings gap narrowed by a large margin between 1976 and 1986, the earnings differential remained significant and pervasive. The female/male income ratio stabilized at about two-thirds after 1986 (see Lui and Suen 1993, 1994 for further discussions). Men earned an average of HK$8,818 per month in 1991 (at current market prices), which is eight times the amount they earned in 1976. In real terms, average main employment income more than doubled during the reported period. The rate of growth of main employment income was higher for women than it was for men. Working women's average monthly income rose from HK$683 in 1976 to HK$5,984 in 1991 (at current market prices). Since female workers' income increased at a fast rate, the gender earnings gap shrunk considerably during the period.

    In terms of schooling, men on average received 7.4 years of education in 1976, about one more year than women received.

Table 3.3

Socioeconomic Characteristics of Male and Female Workers

(A) Males

Characteristics (Variables)	1976	1981	1986	1991
Age	36.0	35.1	35.8	36.8
Years of schooling	7.4	7.9	8.7	9.2
Years of working experience	22.6	21.2	21.1	21.6
Main employment income ($)	1,120	2,272	4,126	8,818
Marital status (%)				
Single	38.1	40.2	37.6	34.8
Married	60.1	58.3	60.4	63.6
Separated / Widowed	1.8	1.6	1.9	1.6
Place of birth (%)				
Hong Kong	37.2	43.1	51.2	55.9
China (including Macau)	59.0	53.1	45.2	39.2
Others	3.7	3.8	3.6	5.0

(B) Females

Age	31.0	31.3	32.7	33.3
Years of schooling	6.6	7.75	8.7	9.6
Years of working experience	18.5	17.8	18.1	17.8
Main employment income ($)	683	1,472	2,788	5,984
Marital status (%)				
Single	53.6	49.5	44.9	42.1
Married	41.7	45.7	50.4	54.0
Separated / Widowed	4.8	4.8	4.7	3.9
Place of birth (%)				
Hong Kong	56.1	57.6	61.1	62.4
China (including Macau)	41.8	38.4	33.6	28.2
Others	2.1	4.0	5.4	9.4

Notes: Calculations are based on 1% census files.

However, female workers overtook their male counterparts in 1991, when they received 0.4 more years of schooling. One may be surprised that females received more education than males did, on average. Readers should be reminded that Table 3.3 summarizes information about the working population and not about the population as a whole. If we look at the whole economy, we would see different patterns. The labour force participation rate of men of prime working age is typically above 90%. Thus, the socio-economic characteristics of working men are largely the same as are those of men in the economy as a whole. On the other hand, the rate of female participation in the labour force was only 50% in 1991. Those women who chose to work in the labour market tended to have better earning potential than did their male counterparts. According to the human capital theory, women with a higher level of education (investment in education) command a higher income than do those with less education. Therefore, educated women are more likely to work in the labour market than are uneducated ones. In the economic literature, this is often referred to as a self-selectivity problem or a sample selection problem (see, for example, Heckman 1979 and Killingsworth 1983 for further discussion). In short, the mean characteristics of working women presented in Table 3.3 (B) does not accurately reflect the characteristics women in the economy as a whole.

When we talk about the female labour supply in Hong Kong, we should include foreign domestic helpers in our discussion. Suen (1994) clearly shows that employing domestic helpers can bring about substantial gains. The presence of a domestic helpers partially releases married women, and to a lesser extent, married man from their family responsibilities. A lot of families in Hong Kong employ live-in domestic helpers. Local workers who have their own families in Hong Kong are not particularly interested in being live-in domestic helpers. As a result, Hong Kong has allowed a large number of foreign workers to enter the country to serve this function. The number of foreign domestic helpers in Hong Kong has increased substantially in the last two decades, rising from 1,350 in 1975 to more than 70,000 in 1990 (Ho et al. 1991). This increase also explains the reason behind the big jump in the number of female workers born outside Hong Kong as detailed in Table 3.3 (B). Moreover, because of the tightened immigration policy, there were proportionally more native workers, both male and female, in the labour market in 1991 than there were in 1976.

Since the socioeconomic characteristics of working men and women are so different, it makes sense to separate them into two groups in order to analyze their respective income distributions. In Table 3.4, I present various commonly used measures of income

Table 3.4
Measures of Income Inequality of Male and Female Workers

(A) Males

Inequality Indicators	1976	1981	1986	1991
Gini coefficient	0.374	0.381	0.407	0.424
Coefficient of variation	1.309	1.424	1.300	1.205
Log income				
Mean	6.775	7.475	8.042	8.781
Variance	0.376	0.386	0.438	0.481
Quantile ratio				
P_{90}/P_{75}	1.591	1.458	1.750	1.667
P_{90}/P_{50}	2.188	2.059	2.333	2.500
P_{90}/P_{10}	3.500	3.553	4.667	5.000
P_{70}/P_{25}	1.833	2.000	2.000	2.093
P_{50}/P_{25}	1.333	1.417	1.500	1.395
P_{50}/P_{10}	1.600	1.726	2.000	2.000

(B) Females

	1976	1981	1986	1991
Gini coefficient	0.314	0.340	0.370	0.383
Coefficient of variation	0.995	1.199	0.987	1.050
Log income				
Mean	6.345	7.091	7.698	8.449
Variance	0.318	0.347	0.416	0.421
Quantile ratio				
P_{90}/P_{75}	1.429	1.667	1.667	1.692
P_{90}/P_{50}	1.818	2.083	2.500	2.485
P_{90}/P_{10}	3.333	3.846	5.000	4.889
P_{70}/P_{25}	1.556	1.667	1.875	2.167
P_{50}/P_{25}	1.222	1.333	1.250	1.476
P_{50}/P_{10}	1.833	1.846	2.000	1.968

Note: Calculations are based on 1% census files.

inequality of male and female workers. The Gini coefficient for men was similar to that for the whole working population. The co-efficient was slightly above 0.37 and 0.38 for 1976 and 1981, respectively. It increased to 0.407 in 1986 and rose further to 0.424 in 1991. I depict the Lorenz curves for men for 1976 and 1991 in

Figure 3.4 (A). The figure indicates that income inequality increased over time, and the Lorenz curve for 1991 lies entirely below that for 1976. The bottom quartile of male workers accounted for 11% of the total product in 1976, but its share fell to 9% in 1991. On the other hand, the top quartile of working men earned 52% of the total product in 1976, and the percentage rose to 56 in 1991. If we look at the higher-income earners, the top decile accounted for 33% and 36% of Hong Kong's total income in 1976 and 1991, respectively. In other words, one third of the total income went into the pockets of one tenth of the working men.

The variance of log income and all quantile ratios for men tells the same story as does the Gini coefficient. A substantial jump in the variance of log income was recorded in the period between 1976 and 1991. The variance was only 0.376 in 1976, but it surged to 0.481 in 1991, an increase of 28%. Similarly, all quantile ratios presented in Table 3.4 (A) reported an increase. The ratio of the median over the last decile experienced the highest increase, rising 25% from 1976 to 1991. On the other hand, the ratio of the median over the first quarter rose by less than 5% in the same period. In short, income inequality among working men was higher in 1991 than that it was in 1976, and income dispersion also increased in the same period.

From Table 3.4 (B), we can see that the inequality in the income distribution of working women was much lower than was that of working men. The Gini coefficient for women was smaller than was that for men during the same year. If the proportion of working women in the labour market increases, the income inequality of the whole working population can decrease, other things being equal. Nevertheless, the Gini coefficient for female workers also increased, from 0.314 in 1976 to 0.383 in 1991. In order to give a better sense of the income distribution during this period, I plot the Lorenz curves for working women for 1976 and 1991 in Figure 3.4 (B). As it does in Figure 3.4 (A), in Figure 3.4 (B) the Lorenz curve for 1991 lies entirely below that for 1976. For example, the first decile of female workers only accounted for 3% of the total income for both 1976 and 1991. In other words, as far as the bottom 10% of the

Figure 3.4
Lorenz Curves for Males and Females

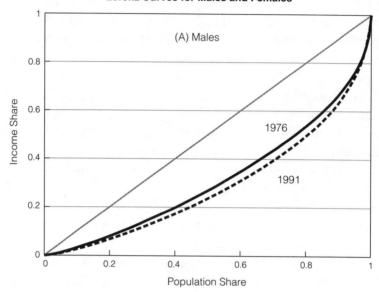

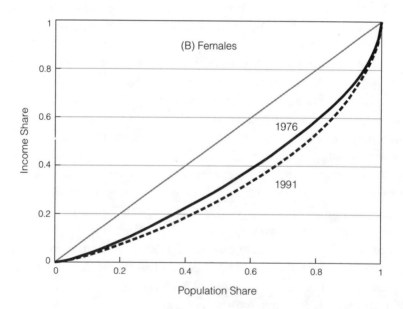

female working population is concerned, income inequality remained unchanged over time. However, when we look at the first quarter, this group earned 12% of the total income in 1976, and the percentage dropped to 10 in 1991. The picture is very different if we study the income share of the last quarter. The top-earning 25% of working women only accounted for 47% of the total income in 1976, but the percentage rose to 52 in 1991. It is evident that during the period income dispersion for women widened and inequality in income distribution increased.

From Table 3.4 (B), we can see that all quantile ratios increased in the period from 1976 to 1991. These ratios show that income dispersion widened. Other measures of income inequality for female workers are rather consistent with this finding. While the coefficient of variation for 1976 rose slightly in 1991, the variance of log income reported a noticeable increase in the same period. To sum up, inequality of income distribution for working men and women seemed greater in 1991 than it did in 1976. This is in line with the situation for the whole working population.

Income Distribution of Households

In all societies, and in Chinese societies in particular, the family has always been one of the most important social institutions. The Chinese take kinship seriously. It is extremely common for sons and daughters to transfer cash to their parents at regular intervals, normally on a monthly basis. This continues even after a child has reached adulthood and has his/her own nuclear family. Moreover, they are ready to share their resources with family members if and when necessary. Hong Kong's population is predominantly Chinese, and family is of prime importance. Thus, it is vital to consider the transfer of cash and in kind when we are studying income distribution of households in the territory. As far as the distribution of command over resources is concerned, it is appropriate to consider the family as the basic unit of analysis.

In principle, we should include the potential income of non-working family members, and non-working wives in particular, when we analyze household income distribution. Pong (1989) shows that a wife's earnings has an equalizing effect on observed family income distribution. This finding is consistent with research done in the U.S., which suggests that working wives tend to equalize household income distribution, especially among white families (see for example, Smith 1979 and Danziger 1980). In studying the distribution of potential income, economists typically use the Heckman (1979) type of sample selection corrected estimation method to compute the reservation wage for non-working females. Along these lines, Pong (1989) constructs the distribution of po- tential family earnings and suggests that if all wives worked in the labour market, income inequality across families would decrease. In this book, I focus only on the distribution of observed income.

A family may consist of several households living in different parts in Hong Kong. Unfortunately, family data is not available, and researchers have to resort to household data included in a 1% random sub-sample of the population census made available by the government. Thus, the reported inequality measures have to be interpreted with care, especially when the composition of a typical household has changed over time. As a matter of fact, average household size has decreased continuously in the last few decades, not only in Hong Kong but in most other developed economies, as well. In 1961 the average number of members in a household in Hong Kong was 4.4. The number decreased to 4.2 in 1976 (Census & Statistics Department 1978). If we look at more recent census reports, we can observe an unmistakable downward trend in average household size. In 1981 a household on average had 3.9 members, and the mean household size decreased further to 3.4 in 1991 (Census & Statistics Department 1993).

Aging populations and lowering fertility rates are major con- cerns of governments of many developed and developing countries. Wise (1990, 1992, 1994) collects papers presented in conferences on the economics of aging organized by the National Bureau of Eco- nomic Research. Caldwell (1984) documents various theories of fertility decline. Davis et al. (1987) focus on the alarmingly low fer- tility rate in industrial societies. Coale and Watkins (1986) edit the proceedings concentrating on the decline of fertility in Europe. The fertility rate in Hong Kong is among the lowest in the world, and it is well below the replacement level. Researchers such as Lowe (1980) and Siu (1988) study family structure and fertility in Hong Kong. However, these issues are not the foci of this book, and I will not discuss them further.

From the four 1% census files, one can ascertain that a small number of households in Hong Kong earned no income in the census reference month. On average, these "no-income" house-holds are much smaller than are other households. The former have less than 3 members, on average, none of whom are employed. In 1991 twenty households earned zero income, and the average number of members in these households was less than 1.8. In 1976, 4.6% of households earned zero income in the census reference month. A significant portion of these households were not genuine zero-income families. In the 1976 by-census incomes were counted de facto, whereas in 1971 census incomes were counted de jure. Those households whose only income earners were not in the household on the census reference night were excluded from the calculation of household income (Census & Statistics Department 1978). The presence of such households in the data set will lead to an overestimation of income inequality. It also explains why the Gini coefficients presented in Table 3.5 (A) were higher than were the corresponding official estimates and those in Table 3.5 (B). Moreover, when we analyze the income distribution of households in Hong Kong, the variance of the logarithmic income cannot be applied to a sample of households with zero income. This is simply because log(0) is undefined in mathematics. To get around this problem I remove zero-income households from the data set when I compute the variance of log income. As a matter of fact, the government also excludes these households from the data set when computing the Gini coefficient. For comparison purposes, I will exclude zero-income households in subsequent analyzes in this book.

The basic characteristics of all Hong Kong households and of the sub-sample of households with positive income are presented in Table 3.5. From Table 3.5 (A), we can see that the average

Chapter 3

Table 3.5
Characteristics and Inequality Measures of Households

(A) All Households

Variables and Indicators	1976	1981	1986	1991
Household size	4.22	4.11	3.69	3.45
Household income	1,902	4,035	7,202	14,238
Income per household member	450	982	1,951	4,122
Zero income household (%)	4.6	0.2	0.0	0.1
Gender of household head (%)				
Male	72.2	74.5	73.9	75.9
Female	27.8	25.5	26.1	24.1
Gini coefficient	0.473	0.453	0.443	0.458
Coefficient of variation	1.756	1.374	1.135	1.049
Quantile ratio				
P_{90}/P_{75}	1.624	1.558	1.639	1.647
P_{90}/P_{50}	2.563	2.534	2.740	2.800
P_{90}/P_{10}	8.047	7.400	6.850	8.252
P_{75}/P_{25}	2.663	2.639	2.652	2.833
P_{50}/P_{25}	1.688	1.622	1.586	1.667
P_{50}/P_{10}	3.140	2.920	2.500	2.947

(B) Households with Positive Income

Household size	4.32	4.11	3.69	3.46
Household income	1,995	4,045	7,214	14,256
Income per household member	462	984	1,953	4,124
Gender of household head (%)				
Male	73.6	74.5	74.0	75.9
Female	26.4	25.5	26.0	24.1
Gini coefficient	0.447	0.452	0.442	0.457
Coefficient of variation	1.701	1.371	1.133	1.048
Log Income				
Mean	7.241	7.922	8.530	9.170
Variance	0.630	0.779	0.710	0.873
Quantile ratio				
P_{90}/P_{75}	1.591	1.558	1.633	1.647
P_{90}/P_{50}	2.500	2.517	2.740	2.800
P_{90}/P_{10}	5.833	7.400	6.850	8.235
P_{75}/P_{25}	2.444	2.639	2.623	2.833
P_{50}/P_{25}	1.556	1.633	1.563	1.667
P_{50}/P_{10}	2.333	2.940	2.500	2.941

Note: Calculations are based on 1%census files.

household size decreased markedly in the period 1976 to 1991. In 1976 the average number of members in a household was 4.22, and the number fell to 3.45 in 1991, which represents a decrease of 0.77 household member. These figures are in line with the official statistics published in various census reports.

Average household income increased more than seven times between 1976 and 1991. At current market prices, the mean household income was under HK$2,000 in 1976, and it had increased to more than HK$14,000 by 1991. The increase in the level of household income was of the same magnitude as was the increase in personal main employment income. However, household size was much smaller in 1991 than it was in 1976. If we take into account the changes in household size, household income increased faster than personal income did during the period. In Table 3.5, I present income per household member by dividing mean household income by average household size. The average household income per member was HK$450 in 1976, and it had increased nine times to HK$4,122 by 1991. The pattern of the increase in income of all households shown in Table 3.5 (A) was essentially the same as was that of households with positive incomes presented in Table 3.5 (B).

In 1996 Hong Kong's divorce procedures were substantially streamlined. It is expected that the divorce rate will increase further due to the fact that it has become easier to apply for the dissolution of marriage. The number of reported divorce cases increased from 5,047 in 1985 to 9,272 in 1994 (Census & Statistics Department 1995). Divorced women are more likely to be household heads, and the number of single-parent households may affect overall income distribution in Hong Kong. Bearing this in mind, I compute the percentage share of households headed by males and females in Table 3.5. Contrary to general belief, the percentage share of female household heads declined from 26.4% in 1976 to 24.1% in 1991. One possible explanation for this may be that women live with their parents when they get divorced. Thus, the higher rate of marriage dissolution would have no apparent impact on the percentage share of female household heads. If we exclude zero-income households, Table 3.5 (B) shows that the portion of households headed by females decreased slightly during the period. In other words, a comparatively higher percentage of zero-income households were headed by females.

From Table 3.5 (A), we can see that the Gini coefficient of all households in 1976 was 0.473, the highest coefficient among the four census years. In 1991 the Gini coefficient was 0.458, 0.015 lower than it was in 1976. Although the inequality of personal main employment income distribution has risen over time, household income inequality clearly decreased. The decrease in income inequality reported in Table 3.5 (A) is inconsistent with official statistics. However, the high Gini coefficient for 1976 was due to a relatively large proportion of zero-income households in the data set. In 1976, 4.6% of households had zero income, as compared to no more than 0.2% of zero-income families in other census years. As the government removed such families from the data set when calculating the Gini coefficient, the higher coefficient in Table 3.5 (A) was due entirely to differing sample selection criteria.

A better way to study the trend in the level of household income inequality is to look at samples of households with positive incomes. If we look at the Gini coefficients for households with positive incomes, we can see that income inequality increased in the period 1976 to 1991. Moreover, the coefficient of variation has decrease markedly over the years. The decreasing coefficient of variation is inconsistent with other income inequality measures. This anomalous phenomenon is mainly due the fact that the mean income rose faster than the standard deviation of income did during the period.

Another way of looking at income distribution is to study the quantile ratio. The pattern revealed by the set of quantile ratios presented in Table 3.5 (A) is rather inconclusive. While the first and last ratios decreased from 1976 to 1991, the middle three ratios increased over that time. However, the quantile ratio P_{90}/P_{10} indicates that income levels became increasingly disparate during the period. Furthermore, when we focus on households with positive incomes, a clear pattern emerged. All reported quantile ratios increased during the period. This suggests that income levels were becoming increasingly disparate. The variance of log income tells the same story as do quantile ratios. On the other hand, if we compare the results in Table 3.5 with those in Table 3.2, we notice that the Gini coefficient of households is much higher than is that of the working population. Moreover, the variance of log household is also higher than is the variance of log personal income. In other words, the distribution of household income is more unequal than is the distribution of personal income.

Income Distribution of Natives and Chinese Immigrants

Throughout the history of Hong Kong, Chinese immigrants have constituted a sizable portion of the population, and only a small percentage of Hong Kong natives are not of Chinese origin. Together, Hong Kong natives and Chinese immigrants represent well over 90% of the population. Foreign workers only accounted for 6.6% of Hong Kong's working population (see Table 3.1) in 1991. Typically, foreign workers are concentrated in selected industries and occupations. Excluding foreign domestic helpers, they earn much more than do average workers in Hong Kong. Because of the sheer number of people in Hong Kong who are Chinese by origin, readers may be wish to know more about the income distribution of natives and Chinese immigrants. In this section, I single out natives and Chinese immigrants from the working population and analyze their income distribution.

Table 3.6 summarizes the characteristics of this sub-sample (which excludes foreign workers) and presents various measures of income inequality. In the four census years, the mean ages of subjects in the sub-sample ranged from 33.7 to 35.4. In 1976 their average number of years of schooling was 7.1, but it rose to 9.2 in 1991. In other words, an average local worker received a lower-secondary education in 1991. Bearing in mind that older, less-educated workers were still working in the labour market, the fact

Table 3.6

Characteristics and Inequality Measures of Chinese

Variables and Indicators	1976	1981	1986	1991
Age	34.4	33.7	34.6	35.4
Years of schooling	7.1	7.6	8.5	9.2
Years of working experience	21.4	20.1	20.1	20.3
Main employment income ($)	939	1,891	3,490	7,502
Gender (%)				
Male	68.1	66.0	64.3	63.6
Female	31.9	34.0	35.7	36.4
Gini coefficient	0.355	0.355	0.383	0.395
Coefficient of variation	1.190	1.189	1.151	1.104
Log income				
Mean	6.228	7.326	7.905	8.658
Variance	0.370	0.370	0.428	0.443
Quantile ratio				
P_{90}/P_{75}	1.500	1.500	1.579	1.563
P_{90}/P_{50}	2.143	2.000	2.308	2.273
P_{90}/P_{10}	3.750	3.750	4.444	4.167
P_{75}/P_{25}	2.000	2.000	1.979	2.000
P_{50}/P_{25}	1.400	1.500	1.354	1.375
P_{50}/P_{10}	1.750	1.875	1.926	1.833

Note: Calculations are based on 1% census files.

that the average number of years of schooling rose by 2.1 years implies a much greater increase in the number of years that younger workers attended school. The average main employment income increased eight times between 1976 and 1991. If we study the composition of female workers, we will notice that the larger share of female workers in the labour market was due to rising labour-force participation of female Chinese immigrants. In the second part of this section, I divide the sub-sample into two groups, natives and Chinese immigrants, and further discuss the issue of female labour-force participation.

As in the previous section, I also present various measures of income inequality of all Chinese workers in Table 3.6. As expected, the Gini coefficient increased markedly over the period. Different income inequality indicators suggest that inequality in income distribution for 1976 was similar to that of 1981. However, there was a clear upward trend after 1981. The coefficient for native and

Table 3.7
Characteristics and Inequality Measures by Place of Birth

(A) Natives

Variables and Indicators	1976	1981	1986	1991
Age	25.9	27.1	29.0	31.1
Years of schooling	8.3	8.7	9.6	10.1
Years of working experience	11.7	12.4	13.4	14.9
Main employment income ($)	915	1,893	3,634	8,161
Gender (%)				
Male	59.1	59.1	59.7	59.8
Female	40.9	40.9	40.3	40.2
Gini coefficient	0.374	0.353	0.379	0.395
Coefficient of variation	1.201	1.028	1.057	1.091
Log income				
Mean	6.577	7.333	7.953	8.743
Variance	0.393	0.364	0.422	0.439

(B) Chinese Immigrants

Age	41.3	40.3	42.0	42.7
Years of schooling	6.1	6.5	7.1	7.6
Years of work experience	29.2	27.8	28.9	29.1
Main employment income ($)	958	1,889	3,297	6,406
Gender (%)				
Male	75.4	72.8	70.4	69.8
Female	24.6	27.2	29.6	30.2
Gini coefficient	0.337	0.357	0.386	0.381
Coefficient of variation	1.168	1.331	1.283	1.094
Log income				
Mean	6.660	7.320	7.840	8.516
Variance	0.348	0.377	0.429	0.416

Note: Calculations are based on 1% census files.

Chinese immigrant workers in Hong Kong was 0.355 in 1981, and it rose to 0.395 in 1991. Other measures of inequality in income distribution tell essentially the same story as does the Gini coefficient. The variance in log income increased by 20% in the ten years between 1981 and 1991. Regarding the set of quantile ratios shown in Table 3.6, five of the six ratios recorded an increase from 1976 to 1991. All these indices point to the same conclusion, that

Figure 3.5
Gini Coefficient by Place of Birth

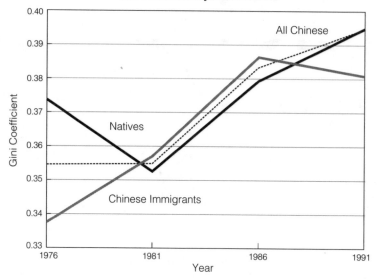

income inequality was more pronounced in 1991 than it was in 1976.

Most people would expect the socio-economic characteristics of natives to be very different from those of Chinese immigrants. For this reason, I tabulate their characteristics and various inequality measures of the two groups in Table 3.7. I also plot the Gini coefficients of natives, Chinese immigrants, and the pooled sample of the four census years in Figure 3.5. The dotted line in Figure 3.5 refers to the Gini coefficient of the pooled sample, i.e. natives and Chinese immigrants. In 1976 income inequality among Chinese immigrants was the least pronounced, whereas the Gini coefficient for native workers was the highest. Moreover, all three lines in Figure 3.5 cluster around the number 0.355 in 1981. In other words, the Gini coefficients for the three groups were very close to each other in 1981. The convergence of these three lines indicates that income inequality among Chinese immigrants increased during the period, while the income of native workers was more evenly distributed in 1981 than it was earlier.

Between 1981 and 1986 all three lines moved in the same direction and in the same order of magnitude. Nevertheless, the pattern observed in 1976 reappeared in 1991. Income inequality among native workers was the highest, whereas among Chinese immigrants it was the lowest. On the one hand, the incomes of immigrants from China are often lower than are those of native workers, causing income levels to be more disparate, overall. On the other hand, the incomes of Chinese immigrants are less disparate than are those of native workers, and the presence of the former group in the labour market has a dampening effect on overall income inequality. Lam (1995) decomposes the variance in log income of Hong Kong for the period 1981 to 1991. She argues that the increase in income inequality over time is mainly due to the increase in within-group inequality. In other words, the observed increase in income inequality is due to the increase in income dispersion within various immigrant groups. She also concludes that if we remove new Chinese immigrants from the population, the observed disparity in income levels is lower.

To understand more about Hong Kong natives and Chinese immigrants, we can look at Table 3.7. The characteristics and the income inequality measure of native workers are presented in Table 3.7 (A), and information related to Chinese immigrants is given in Table 3.7 (B). Native workers are much younger than are immigrants from China. In 1976 native workers, on average, were only 25.9 years old — more than 15 years younger than their immigrant counterparts. The average age of natives was experiencing a rising trend, and it increased steadily from 1976 to 1991. On the other hand, the average age of Chinese immigrants remained rather stable over the period. By 1991 the age gap had been reduced to 11.6 years. Since Chinese immigrants were much older than their native Hong Kong counterparts, they had more work experience. On average, the length of their work experience was around twenty-eight to twenty-nine years. The mean length of native workers' work experience, on the other hand, was only 11.7 years in 1976, and it rose to 14.9 years in 1991.

In terms of years of schooling, native workers have a clear advantage over immigrant workers. In any census year shown in Table 3.7, native workers received 2 to 2.5 more years of schooling than did Chinese immigrants. According to the human capital theory, natives should thus earn more than immigrants from China do, other things being equal. If we focus on work experience, Chinese immigrants should earn more than natives do. Since these two factors work in opposing directions, it is not clear which group will earn more. From Table 3.7, we can see that the immigrant-native income ratio was close to 1 for 1976 and for 1981. However, the income gap widened after 1986, and the immigrant-native income ratio dropped to 0.78 in 1991. Lui and Suen (1996) argue that quality of education does help to explain the immigrant-native income gap. The percentage share of female workers within the two groups was also clearly different. Female workers consistently accounted for two-fifths of the native workforce. The ratio of female to male workers among immigrants from China was much lower than was the corresponding ratio among native workers. As females workers earn less on average than do male workers, the lower the percentage share of female workers, the higher the average income. In other words, the lower immigrant-native income ratio is partly due to the rising portion of female immigrant workers. If the percentage share continues to increase, the observed immigrant-native income ratio will decrease further, other things being equal.

Another way to measure the income gap is to compute the difference in mean log income. From Table 3.7, we can see that the difference in mean log income for 1991 is 0.227, which indicates that immigrants from China, on average, earned 22.7 log points less than natives do. In Table 3.7, I also present the Gini coefficient and the coefficient of variation of the two groups. In order not to overwhelm readers with numbers, I choose not to present quantile ratios here. The changes in the variance of log income were similar to the changes in the Gini coefficient. The recorded variance of log income for Chinese immigrants in 1976 was much lower than was that of natives. The difference in the variance of log income narrowed between 1981 and 1986. Moreover, between 1986 and

1991 the variance of log income of natives increased from 0.422 to 0.439. In the same period, the variance of log income for Chinese immigrants decreased from 0.429 to 0.416. In short, the distribution of income for natives and Chinese immigrants were more unequal in 1991 than it was in 1976.

Notes

1. Cowell (1995) demonstrates that comparability and measurability are two are mutually independent characteristics. Readers can refer to Cowell's book for sample cases that are measurable but not comparable and comparable but not measurable.

2. Chapter 3 of Cowell's (1995) book summarizes the characteristics of 13 different measures of income inequality. Readers who want to know which income distribution measures satisfy the four elementary conditions discussed in this book may refer to his book.

3. Suppose there are n persons (or households) in a particular population, and the income y of a person (or a household) i is expressed as y_i. A formal definition of the Gini coefficient is:

$$\text{Gini coefficient} = \frac{1}{2n^2\overline{Y}}\sum_{i=1}^{n}\sum_{j=1}^{n}\left|y_i - y_j\right|$$

4. See Ho et al. (1991) for an interesting discussion of emigration in and out of Hong Kong since 1950. The authors provide a detailed account of different phases of the changing immigration policy.

CHAPTER 4

Education and Public Housing Policies

Public policies by their nature affect the public at large. Some public policies in Hong Kong have more of a direct impact on the distribution of income in Hong Kong than others do. Policies such as the education policy, the public housing policy, the health care policy, and the social welfare policy all affect the distribution of income. The taxation system affects it as well. In this book, I limit my discussion of public policy to the areas of education and housing.

Education policies have pronounced effects on income distribution because they affect educational opportunities which influence earning ability. The human capital theory suggests that the higher the educational level of a worker, the higher will be his or her labour earnings.

Housing is a major concern of people the world over. In Hong Kong, households living in public housing estates receive government subsidies in the form of reduced rent. So public housing subsidies must be taken into account in analysis of household income distribution.

An economy's taxation system not only directly affects the purchasing power of individuals but also affects disposable income of households. Ho (1979) studies the distribution of the tax burden and public expenditure benefits among Hong Kong households by income group. His analysis is based on a sample survey of 1,500 households conducted in June 1970. After deducting all taxes, the estimated Gini coefficient was 0.39, as opposed to the raw official estimate of 0.41. Thus, Hong Kong's taxation system did lower the inequality of income distribution. Since the taxation system has remained much the same as it was in 1970, Ho's analysis should still apply today.

The social welfare policy and the health care policy are two other public policies that affect income distribution through the "redistributive effect" on income. Unfortunately, there is as yet no suitable data source which can help identify the beneficiaries of social welfare services and medical and health services. A possible way in which to analyze the impact of taxation and other policies on income distribution would be to conduct a dedicated survey for this purpose. This kind of survey has not been conducted in Hong Kong. Instead, for now, I focus on the relations between income distribution and education and public housing policies. In order to account for the true extent of public housing subsidies that have been received by public housing tenants, I employ two simple methods to arrive at an adjusted household income distribution. In the next section, I briefly review the public expenditure by major functional components in Hong Kong. Then follows the section on the relations between education policies and income distribution. The housing policies aspects of income distribution constitute the last section of this chapter.

Public Expenditure

The Hong Kong government is the largest employer in the economy, and its policies directly impact not only civil servants but also local workers. For example, the government is determined to raise the educational level of the general public, and to this end it has provided education to school children since 1971. Legislation on compulsory education for children aged six to fourteen went into effect in 1980. The education policy has played a crucial part in making upward social mobility possible in Hong Kong. The recent expansion of tertiary education opportunities in the territory has further fuelled the push for increased social mobility.

Regarding Hong Kong's fiscal system, the government is committed to a "balanced-budget" policy. Before the implementation of the port and airport projects in the 1990s, public expenditure seldom exceeded government revenue. Over the years, public expenditure has constituted less than one-fifth of Hong Kong's gross domestic product. Although the size of the public sector is relatively small by international standards, its activities cover a wide spectrum of public services. In general, these services are of high quality and are made available to all citizens at nominal charges. Law and order are enforced by a diligent and modernized police force. The legal framework protects all individuals on an equal basis. Most importantly, in the eyes of economists, the government cultivates a business environment that promotes free trade. It sets no trade barriers, and Hong Kong markets are opened to the world at large.

Public expenditure comprises of the following components (Finance Branch 1996):

1. Trading funds;
2. Hong Kong Housing Authority;
3. Urban Council and the Regional Council;
4. All expenditures financed by the government's statutory funds; and
5. All expenditures charged to the General Revenue Account.

The General Revenue Account records moneys collected by the government and appropriations of expenditure as stipulated in various ordinances (Hong Kong Annual Digest of Statistics 1995). Expenditures by institutions in the private and quasi-private sector are included as public expenditure to the extent of their subventions (Finance Branch 1996). However, they do not include:

1. expenditure by those statutory and non-statutory organizations in which the government has only an equity position; and
2. advances and equity investments from the Capital Investment Fund.

Table 4.1

Public Expenditure by Functional Component, 1986–1996

Component	1986/87	87/88	88/89	89/90	90/91
Economic	2,525	2,996	3,516	4,065	5,222
Security	7,454	8,090	9,598	11,544	13,843
Social welfare	2,576	2,863	3,485	4,379	5,318
Health	4,366	4,979	5,673	7,254	9,230
Education	8,598	9,450	11,654	13,392	16,542
Environment	397	413	525	1,198	2,025
Community & external affairs	3,279	3,737	4,346	5,387	6,591
Infrastructure	6,707	7,406	8,783	13,960	11,943
Support	6,244	6,672	7,464	9,196	12,067
Housing	5,785	7,032	9,755	11,569	12,416
Public expenditure	47,930	53,636	64,799	81,945	95,198

	1991/92	92/93	93/94	94/95	95/96#
Economic	5,849	7,563	12,447	7,374	9,637
Security	14,899	16,286	17,322	18,975	21,323
Social welfare	6,352	7,299	9,170	10,948	14,558
Health	10,693	13,636	18,458	19,322	23,852
Education	19,431	22,158	25,409	28,878	33,781
Environment	2,675	3,129	3,134	4,401	6,167
Community & external affairs	6,754	6,973	8,326	9,229	11,006
Infrastructure	14,279	17,484	23,051	26,231	27,040
Support	14,504	16,034	21,284	20,891	26,621
Housing	12,577	12,932	16,607	19,701	21,259
Public expenditure	108,012	123,493	155,207	165,950	195,245

Source: Finance Branch, Government Secretariat, 1996
Notes: All figures are expressed in HK$ Million at current market prices.
          # Revised estimates.

Based on this definition, expenditures of organizations such as the Mass Transit Railway Corporation, the Kowloon Canton Railway Corporation, and the Airport Authority are excluded.

Broadly speaking, public expenditure in Hong Kong can be classified into ten functional components. Among these ten functional components, public spending on education, housing, and social services (including social welfare and health services) are the main vehicles by which the government redistributes wealth within the society. Table 4.1 presents the distribution of public expenditure by functional component for the fiscal years 1986/87 to 1995/96. These figures are routinely published in the annual Budget Speech when the Financial Secretary tables the government budget to the Legislative Council for deliberation. Over the years, there have been a number of changes in the functional breakdown, and the breakdown for earlier years differs substantially from the one presented in Table 4.1. For instance, items such as "General Services" were dropped and new functions such as "Environment" and "Support" were added to the functional breakdown. A direct comparison of functional expenditure over more than ten years would therefore be misleading.[1]

Looking at Table 4.1, we can see that spending on the "environment" function has increased the most. This new function was added to the breakdown beginning in the 1985/1986 fiscal year. The government has done a lot of work to improve Hong Kong's living environment, for example by establishing the Environmental Protection Department. A major task of the department is to encourage people not to pollute the environment. Although the results of its effort have yet to be seen, the public has begun to be aware of the importance of protecting the environment.

The government has also invested a huge sum of money in restructuring the public health services system, which has led to increased spending on the "health" function. The most noticeable change in the system is that all government hospitals are now under the auspices of the Hospital Authority. The Hospital Authority is not a government department and has full autonomy in its operation. As the Authority has only been established for a few years, we should expect higher capital investment for some years to come. Thus, public spending on the "health" function is expected to continue to increase. The data in Table 4.1 confirms this conjecture.

Anyone interested in Hong Kong's education system would remember the hot debate in the late 1980s over the construction of a new university, now the Hong Kong University of Science and Technology. In late 1994 three tertiary institutions, the then Hong

Figure 4.1
Distribution of Public Expenditure

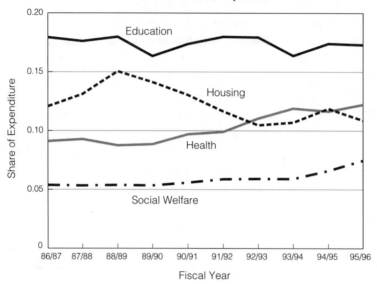

Source: Finance Branch, Government Secretariat, 1996

Kong Polytechnic, the City Polytechnic of Hong Kong, and the
Hong Kong Baptist College, were upgraded to university status.
The move was in line with the development in the early 1990s of the
tertiary education system in the U.K. where almost all polytechnics
and selected post-secondary colleges were upgraded to universities
in the U.K. by 1992. Moreover, the British government is gradually
replacing all non-graduate teachers (in primary and secondary
schools) with graduate teachers who have professional teaching
qualification.[2] The Hong Kong government is following in the
British government's footsteps, but much more slowly.

Such moves to upgrade the quality of education in Hong Kong
have given the general public the impression that the Hong Kong
government has substantially increased education spending; but, in
fact this is not the case. Even though absolute spending on
education has increased, the percentage share of total public
expenditure allocated to education has remained more or less the

same. Figure 4.1 depicts the distribution of public expenditure in four functional components: health, housing, education, and social welfare.

Given the rapid expansion of tertiary education, government spending on this sector has increased drastically, while primary and secondary schools have inevitably received a smaller share of the pie. Numerous commentators have criticized the government for concentrating too much on university education at the expenses of primary and secondary school education. Meanwhile, tertiary institutions face many difficulties in financing their operations. For example, the Chinese University of Hong Kong was forced to restructure its four-year first degree curriculum into a three-year programme due to financial problems. As a result of their financial difficulties, all tertiary institutions seek monetary support from the private sector and actively engage in fund-raising activities. Moreover, tuition is adjusted upward annually at a rate much higher than the rate of inflation. In the 1992–1993 academic year, tuition for a full-time degree programme was HK$11,600, and it increased to HK$37,600 in the 1996–1997 academic year. Students from low-income families may have problems paying tuition. At present, all tertiary institutions allow students to pay their fees in installments. Although students with financial difficulties can seek assistance from the government, interest-free loans are no longer available to them. All these policy changes have long-term effects on the distribution of income.

Education Policy and Income Distribution

The education system in Hong Kong has undergone two major changes in the last two decades. The first of these was the provision of free and universal elementary education in the 1970s and the second was the rapid expansion of tertiary education in the late 1980s. In many developed countries, elementary education is provided by the government for little or no charge; very often, enrolment in elementary school is compulsory. The Hong Kong government started providing free and universal primary education

Table 4.2
International Comparison of Public Expenditure on Education in 1990

Country	As % of GNP	As % of Public Expenditure
Canada	6.8	14.2
China	2.3	12.8
Hong Kong	2.8#	17.4
Japan	4.7	16.5
Korea	4.2*	14.8*
Thailand	3.6	20.0
U. K.	4.9	n.a.
U.S.	5.3	12.3

Sources: UNESCO (1995),
          Census & Statistics Department (1996a)
Notes: #   Figure refers to % of GDP
          *   Figures refer to the year of 1992
          n.a.— Data not available

in 1971 (Census & Statistics Department 1993). In 1978 free and universal education was extended to the junior secondary level. Legislation on compulsory education for children aged six to eleven was enacted in 1971 and was subsequently extended to children up to the age of thirteen and fourteen in 1979 and 1980, respectively. Concurrently, children aged fourteen or below were prohibited by law from taking any form of employment on the labour market.

Before the recent expansion of the tertiary education system occurred, less than one-tenth of youngsters aged seventeen to twenty were able to enter a local university. Since the expansion of the tertiary education system took place, the local degree-conferring institutions jointly have provided first-year first-degree places for 18% of people 17–20 years old.

As discussed in Chapter 2, about 17% of total public expenditure in Hong Kong goes towards education. It would be useful to know the percentages that other economies allocate to education. Table 4.2 presents an international comparison of public expenditure on education in 1990. The first column in the table refers to public expenditure on education as a percentage of an economy's gross national product (GNP), whereas the second column shows public expenditure on education as a percentage of total public expenditure. Not until recently did Hong Kong compile any GNP estimates, and the figure for Hong Kong in the first column is for public expenditure on education as a percentage of GDP. Since the latest statistics show that the ratio of GNP to GDP in Hong Kong is very close to one (see Chapter 2 for further discussion), the figure for Hong Kong in Table 4.2 should be a good indicator of the actual value for comparison purposes.

From Table 4.2, we can see that among the economies in the comparison, Hong Kong spent the second-lowest percentage (2.8%) of its GNP on education. Its percentage share was even lower than was that of Thailand, a developing economy. Japan used 5% of its GNP for education, the highest percentage among the Asian countries. As expected, industrialized economies spent more on education than did newly industrialized and developing economies. Because of the cuts in government subsidies to the education sector in the U.K., it spent only 4.9% of its GNP on education in 1990. China invested only 2.3% of its GNP on education — one of the lowest percentages in the world; in 1993 the percentage share in China decreased further, to 1.9%. This decrease was probably due to many large-scale industrial and other business investment projects undertaken in China at the time.

Hong Kong allocated 17.4% of total public expenditure to education in 1990 (second column of Table 4.2). This percentage share is higher than that of any industrialized economy shown in the table. Surprisingly, the U.S. government came out last in this ranking. Thailand's government made education a very high priority, consistently spending around 20% of its budget on education. In 1980 education accounted for 20.6% of total public expenditure, and the percentage share dropped slightly to 19.6% in 1992. China devoted only 12.8% of the government expenditure pie to education. Numerous researchers (see, for example, Young 1992) indicate that improved labour productivity is the major force behind economic growth. Investment in human capital, i.e., in education, is vital in raising labour productivity.

Despite the lack of natural resources, Hong Kong has managed to achieve continuous and rapid economic growth in the past few decades. Hong Kong's human resources are the key to its success. Hong Kong workers are extremely industrious. They spend a lot of time and energy outside working hours to improve themselves through educational training. A variety of part-time courses at all levels, ranging from introductory Putonghua (Mandarin) to doctoral programmes, are offered by local and overseas institutions (public and private ones).

Investment in infrastructure and other development projects yield immediate but short-term benefits to an economy. We may regard such projects as computer "hardware", human resources being the "software". No matter how superbly hardware is designed or how fast a computer's CPU is, without suitable software one cannot utilize its capabilities. The software, especially the operating system, is the soul of any computer. It is thus advisable for every government to develop a long-term education policy, which I believe will have a long-term positive impact on the economy concerned.

Upgrading of the Workforce

The Hong Kong government is strongly committed to the education system. Public expenditure on education accounts for the largest single item on the fiscal budget. It is a common misconception that the Hong Kong government only provides nine years of free and compulsory education to children aged between six and fifteen. In fact, the government funds education at higher levels as well. Most children in Hong Kong go beyond junior secondary school. It is estimated that about 95% complete upper secondary education (85%), or the equivalent technical education (10%); both streams are highly subsidized (Information Services Department 1996a). After conducting a special review of tertiary education in 1989, the government implemented an ambitious expansion programme at the tertiary level. In the 1994–1995 academic year, local tertiary institutions provided more than 14,000 first-year first-degree places to around 18% of 17–20 years old. The ratio was twice what it was in 1989. If we add sub-degree places, 24% of 17–20 years old had access to tertiary education in 1994–1995.

In addition to increasing access to tertiary education, the government has attempted to improve the education system as a whole. In recent years the Education Department and the University Grants Committee have taken steps to improve the teaching and learning quality at the primary, secondary, and tertiary levels. For example, the government intends to upgrade the quality of primary school teachers, with the goal of filling 35% of the teaching posts at primary schools with university graduates by 2007 (Information Services Department 1996a). The Education Department has also embarked on a Target Oriented Curriculum.

All these measures and the expansion of tertiary education are intended to provide more educational opportunities and higher-quality teaching and learning at all levels. An upgraded workforce has a direct impact on the labour market. Although the results of the recent expansion of tertiary education have yet to be seen, the general upgrading of the workforce in recent past is evident in Table 3.1 and Table 4.3.

In Chapter 3, I state that the average number of years of schooling of workers increased from 7.2 years in 1976 to 9.3 years in 1991. In Table 4.3, (next page) I present the composition of the working population by educational level. In 1976 slightly below 60% of the working population had completed no more than a primary education. When the government started providing free and compulsory primary and junior secondary education in the late 1970s, the general educational standard of the average worker climbed considerably. In 1991, well over 70% of the workforce had gone on to complete at least junior secondary school. In 1976 less than 9% of the working population had completed tertiary level education (post-secondary and degree levels). By 1991 tertiary graduates accounted for 14.6% of the workforce (7.0% plus 7.6%). In fifteen years, the portion of tertiary graduates gained around five percentage points. At the opposite extreme, about 5% of the workforce received no education in 1991, which was 7 percentage points lower than that in 1976. If we look at those with a secondary education, the percentage share doubled, from 16.7% in 1976 to 31.8% in 1991. We can expect continued upgrading of the

Table 4.3
Working Population by Educational Level

Educational Level		1976	1981	1986	1991
No	Age	47.2	47.8	43.5	50.4
Schooling	Female (%)	52.2	55.9	50.7	46.8
	% of Total	12.1	8.8	9.8	4.9
Primary	Age	34.8	36.6	39.7	42.4
	Female (%)	29.6	29.7	30.7	32.4
	% of Total	46.2	36.9	28.1	22.2
Junior	Age	28.7	28.7	30.7	33.7
Secondary	Female (%)	25.2	26.4	25.6	26.8
	% of Total	14.8	20.1	20.2	20.6
Secondary	Age	30.7	28.9	29.9	30.9
	Female (%)	26.8	40.3	42.9	45.2
	% of Total	16.7	22.4	27.9	31.8
Matriculation	Age	28.3	28.4	29.9	2.0
	Female (%)	20.5	31.4	41.3	44.2
	% of Total	1.4	5.0	4.8	5.9
Post-	Age	28.7	33.0	32.9	32.0
Secondary	Female (%)	48.0	44.6	51.4	43.3
	% of Total	4.6	2.6	3.4	7.0
Degree	Age	36.3	37.7	37.2	35.9
	Female (%)	19.9	26.9	29.7	33.3
	% of Total	4.2	4.1	5.8	7.6

Note: Calculations are based on 1% census files.

workforce in the coming years, especially when newly trained university graduates join the labour market.

During 1976–1991 females enjoy more and better education opportunities than they did before, and the improvement in their educational standard was particularly profound. If we look at the four educational sub-groups (secondary and higher) , we can see that the percentage share of females in each sub-group has risen by a large margin. When the first university in Hong Kong opened its door to students, females were simply not eligible to enter. When the economy grew, women gained equal access to education. Before the advent of free and universal public education, education was a luxury good. In a Chinese society like Hong Kong's, parents were more willing to send sons than daughters to school at that time. Nowadays, it is government policy that no one will be denied an education because of lack of means. Students of lower economic status, and female students in particular, are the major beneficiaries of Hong Kong's education policy.

Income Dispersion by Educational Level

The rapid economic growth of Hong Kong has led to marked shifts in the demand for labour (see Chapter 2 for further discussion). Highly skilled workers are now in demand, whereas labour-intensive manufacturing industries have lost their lustre. According to fundamental economic principles, when the demand for skilled workers increases, market forces will push their wage rates up; but if the demand for unskilled labour diminishes, the labour market's invisible hand will suppress unskilled labourers' wages, other things being equal. In short, due to Hong Kong's economic transformation, we should observe increased wage dispersion between educated and uneducated labour.

On the other hand, Hong Kong's education policy aims at upgrading the educational standard of the workforce. The supply of well educated workers has increased over the last two decades. To compare the income changes of workers since the mid-1970s, I use the income of an average secondary school graduate as a reference level to compute the "income ratio". A ratio of 1.5 indicates that the mean income of the respective education sub-group is one and a half times that of the average income of a secondary school graduate. Since secondary school level is used as par value, all income ratios for secondary school level must equal one. In Table 4.4 (A), I use raw income data to compute the income ratios; Table 4.4 (B) presents the more appropriate (adjusted) income ratios which are derived from logarithmic income data. The derivation of income

Chapter 4

Table 4.4
Income Ratio by Educational Level

(A) Raw Income

Educational Level	1976	1981	1986	1991
No schooling	0.577	0.627	0.793	0.543
Primary	0.656	0.739	0.743	0.720
Junior secondary	0.701	0.780	0.786	0.814
Secondary	1.000	1.000	1.000	1.000
Matriculation	1.437	1.314	1.211	1.380
Post-secondary	1.346	1.791	1.893	1.591
Degree	2.806	2.986	2.978	2.887

(B) Logarithmic Income

No schooling	0.810	0.627	0.736	0.564
Primary	0.707	0.798	0.776	0.744
Junior secondary	0.755	0.830	0.832	0.840
Secondary	1.000	1.000	1.000	1.000
Matriculation	1.272	1.203	1.176	1.269
Post-secondary	1.300	1.675	1.827	1.515
Degree	2.230	2.375	2.473	2.285

(C) Income Regressions

No schooling	0.455	0.480	0.442	0.480
Primary	0.584	0.614	0.552	0.531
Junior secondary	0.738	0.740	0.726	0.693
Secondary	1.000	1.000	1.000	1.000
Matriculation	1.340	1.269	1.350	1.359
Post-secondary	1.563	1.748	1.979	1.663
Degree	2.471	2.380	2.714	2.548

Note: Average income of "Secondary" school leavers are taken as the standard (the reference group) in calculating the relative incomes ("income ratios") of other educational groups.

ratios shown in the last panel (C), however, requires separate explanation in the next paragraph.

In economic literature, it is customary to use a human capital "earnings regression" (Mincer 1974), to compute the economic returns to human capital investment in schooling. A major advantage of using an earnings regression is that it can adjust (or "control for variation in") the influence of other variables such as experience and gender. The coefficient estimates derived from an earnings regression can accurately reflect the relationship between income changes ("dependent variables") and the relevant explaining factors ("independent variables"). In this book, I use natural logarithmic income as the dependent variable and other socioeconomic variables. A set of variables about the attributes of education one receives ("dummy variables") as independent variables.[3] The resultant income ratio in Table 4.4 (C) is the best indicator among these three sets of income ratios. This is because the income ratios derived from income regressions are independent of variation in other socioeconomic variables — that is, the ratios in Panel (C) have accounted for the extraneous influences.

Table 4.4 (A) shows that income ratios in 1976 were largely the same as were those in 1991. The ratios in Panel (A) are derived from raw income data and do not take into account individual differences. Degree holders' incomes increased slightly faster than did those of secondary school graduates; uneducated workers enjoyed a slightly slower income increase than did secondary school graduates. Similar patterns also appear in Table 4.4 (B). Both income ratios in Table 4.4 (A) and (B) seem to suggest that the demand side forces discussed earlier were cancelled out by supply side forces. As a result, income growth across different educational levels were in the same order of magnitude. This finding suggests that the supply of and demand for different categories of workers were largely at equilibrium. Lui (1994) also shows that there was no shortfall of graduate workers in the period 1976 to 1991.

Panel (C) presents the change in income ratios in a clearer picture. In the period 1976 to 1991 higher educational groups (i.e. matriculation, post-secondary, and degree levels) experienced slightly faster income growth than did secondary school graduates. Thus, income dispersion widened in that period. As for primary and junior secondary educational groups, their income did not increase as fast as that of the secondary school graduates. Somewhat surprisingly uneducated workers enjoyed a slightly higher rate of income growth than the secondary school graduates.

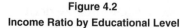

Figure 4.2
Income Ratio by Educational Level

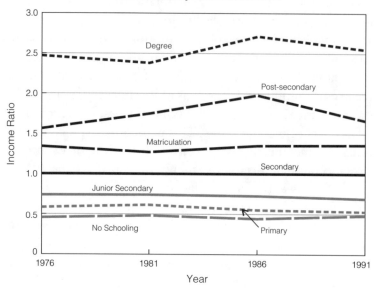

Year

In order to better comprehend the relative growth of the income of different educational groups, I plot the income ratios in panel (C) in Figure 4.2. Workers of matriculation or lower educational levels received similar income adjustments throughout 1976–1991. Thus, the five lines representing these five educational groups are nearly horizontal. The income of the two tertiary educational groups, the post-secondary and the degree level groups, rose faster than average during 1976–1986. However, as more tertiary graduates entered in the labour market, their income level increased the least in the interim. By 1991 the income ratios of these two groups had receded to their 1976 levels. As a whole, better-educated workers received slightly higher income increases than other workers did, but the level of income dispersion among different educational groups remained largely unchanged from 1976 to 1991.

In addition to using a set of education variables which are called "dummies" (or classifiers) as independent variable in human capital earnings regression, economists often use years of schooling as an independent variable.

Another useful result obtained by income regression is the concept of "education premium per additional year of schooling". For example, the coefficient estimate for 1976 is 0.108, which suggests that a worker's income would increase by 10.8% for an additional year of schooling in 1976. The estimated coefficients for the years 1976, 1981, 1986, and 1991 are 0.108, 0.105, 0.130, and 0.132 respectively. Apparently, the education premium had increased over time. Economic transformation in Hong Kong towards a service economy has resulted in a greater demand for skilled labour. Even though the supply of more educated workers rose significantly during 1976–1991, the education premium still increased from 10.8% in 1976 (as noted) to 13.2% in 1991.

There is still one more way of looking at the changes in income dispersion. The composition changes in the dispersion of income is analyzed in terms of the "variance of logarithmic income". The key idea here is that we suspect the variation in (spread of) income inequality *within* different educational groups may differ from the variation in income inequality of the labour force *as a whole*. Furthermore, the extent of inequality may not be the same *between* different educational groups.[4]

Table 4.5 shows that during 1976 and 1991, the income dispersion within the best-educated workers was wider than that of the less-educated groups by a large margin. Broadly speaking, the higher the level of education, the higher the income dispersion within the respective group of workers. The degree of the dispersion (measured by the variance of log income) of uneducated workers was 0.297 in 1976, which was only 38% of that among of graduate workers in the same year (i.e. 0.785 in Table 4.5). By 1991 that percentage had dropped to 35%.

The analysis clearly points out that the change in educational composition of the workforce comes close to explaining all the increases in overall income dispersion (from 0.398 in 1976 to 0.484 in 1991; in Table 4.5, "Overall" row).[5] Had the educational composition of the working population remained unchanged, the

Table 4.5

Decomposition of Income Inequality by Level of Education, 1976–1991

(A) Income Dispersion (variance values)

Educational Level	1976	1981	1986	1991
No schooling	0.297	0.370	0.486	0.308
Primary	0.266	0.272	0.308	0.302
Junior secondary	0.263	0.288	0.279	0.292
Secondary	0.347	0.334	0.340	0.329
Matriculation	0.554	0.438	0.403	0.474
Post-secondary	0.421	0.477	0.479	0.474
Degree	0.785	0.790	0.770	0.891

(B) Sources of Variance of Income Dispersion

	1976	1981	1986	1991
Overall Variance	0.398	0.406	0.457	0.484
Between-group variance	0.082	0.073	0.092	0.108
	(20.7)	(18.1)	(20.0)	(22.4)
Within-group variance	0.316	0.332	0.365	0.376
	(79.3)	(81.9)	(80.0)	(77.6)

(C) Analysis of Change of Inequality during 1976–1991

Change in variance (0.484 minus 0.398, from Panel B)	0.086
Due to composition change	0.081
Between-group	0.046
Within-group	0.035
Due to change in variance	0.005
Between-group	−0.020
Within-group	0.025

Note: Percentage share in parentheses.

income dispersion of Hong Kong workers would only have increased by 0.005 instead of by 0.086, other things being equal. In technical terms, if the distribution of the working population by level of education in 1991 was the same as it was in 1976, the variance of log income would have increased by only 0.005.

It is undeniable that economic restructuring in Hong Kong has led to shifts in labour demand. Although an increasing supply of better-educated workers in the labour market can match the sectoral shifts, the changing the composition of the workforce also caused a 20% increase in dispersion of labour income.

The government policy's of providing more and better educational opportunities to the public at large has been well supported by the changing economic environment, but the statistical evidence shows that it did contribute to the increase of income inequality in Hong Kong. The recent expansion of tertiary education in Hong Kong will lead to a bigger supply of workers with post-secondary and degree education. The income dispersion of highly educated workers is much higher than is that of other workers. On the basis of our analysis about the past, we expect that the expansion of tertiary education will *increase the inequality* of income distribution in the future.

Before I begin the next section on Hong Kong's housing policy and income distribution, I want to point out that the above analysis is a static decomposition of changes in income dispersion. If the composition of the working population had undergone no changes in terms of its educational level, the labour market would respond to sectoral shifts differently. Under these conditions, I believe that the income dispersion between different educational groups would increase even much *faster* than it is increasing now. Moreover, the composition of the working population changed not just in its level of education, but in other dimensions as well. Thus, one should not blame the Hong Kong government's education policy entirely for the rise of income inequality.

Public Housing Policy and Income Distribution

A disastrous fire on Christmas Day 1953 swept the squatter area in Shek Kip Mei and pressed the Hong Kong government to implement its first public housing policy (Fung 1996). Since the inception of the public housing programme in 1954, the Hong Kong government has invested heavily in various types of public housing. The Hong Kong Housing Authority alone provided about 667,000 flats in 155 public rental estates in 1995. At the same time, more than 190,000 flats were sold to local citizens through the Home Ownership Scheme and the Private Sector Participation Scheme (Information Services Department 1996b). In 1995 about

51% of the population or 3.2 million people lived in various types of government-assisted housing — 41% in public rental units and 10% in home-ownership flats.

In the past, public housing was made available only to those in the lower class. In recent years, there has been widespread concern about the housing problems faced by the "sandwich class" — families with income above the qualifying level for cheap public housing but well below the level to afford the expensive private flats. In 1993 the Hong Kong government, through an independent and non-profit-making Housing Society, introduced the Sandwich Class Housing Scheme to provide home purchasing assistance to those families (Information Services Department 1996c). Since another research report in this Series deals with public housing, I will not discuss the public housing policy in detail. Instead, I concentrate on the relations between the public housing policy and income distribution in Hong Kong.[6]

Households living in public housing estates pay below-market-level rents. As these households pay less rent, a greater proportion of their income can be expended for other purposes than can that be spent by those living in private housing. In other words, public housing tenants receive a subsidy from the government. Thus, households living in public housing have higher purchasing power, after deducting rent, than do those households in private housing with the same household income. In analyzing household income distribution, we should make some analytical adjustments by taking into account this kind of government subsidy of households living in public housing. In this section, I propose two income adjustment methods and analyze the adjusted income distribution of households. The Housing Authority often mentions the "median-rent-to-income ratio" in private and public sectors. Moreover, many researchers use this method to adjust the household income. I argue in this section that the income ratio method does not reflect the real picture.

Empirical results show that the public housing programme in Hong Kong could not alleviate income inequality among households. Rich public housing tenants were spending proportionally less on housing than those tenants living in the private sector; on the other hand, poor tenants in public housing estates were found to fare off worse because they spend too much on housing. A few methodological notes are in order before we provide the analytical results in support of the important conclusion stated above.

Income Adjustment Methods

The main objective of the public housing programme in Hong Kong is to bring about social stability (Fung 1996). Hence, public housing must be affordable. When setting rental levels, the Housing Authority will ensure that rents are realistic and sustainable in terms of financial resources. Its rental policy aims at charging rents at a median-rent-to-income ratio not exceeding 15%. On average, public housing tenants pay monthly rent equal to 8.7% of their monthly income, compared with 26% paid by those who live in the private sector (Fung 1996). A household living in private housing earns HK$10,000 a month has to pay HK$2,600 of rent per month on average. If the same household lives in public housing, its monthly rent is only HK$870. The difference of HK$1,730 can be regarded as a government subsidy. This clearly shows that public housing tenants are heavily subsidized by the government.

There are a variety of ways in which to incorporate the government public housing subsidy into the calculation of the adjusted household income. I prefer simple, consistent, and easy-to-implement income adjustment methods to complicated ones.[7] I adopt two income adjustment methods to compute the adjusted household income. The resulting adjusted income distribution derived from these two methods suggests that the public housing subsidy has only a minimal equalizing effect as far as the overall level of income equality in Hong Kong is concerned. I also argue that the regression analysis method is preferable to the income ratio method.[8]

Income Ratio Method

The Housing Authority indicates that on average, households living in public housing estates pay monthly rent equal to 8.7% of their income, whereas households living in private housing pay 26% of their income as rent. The income ratio method assumes that the government public housing subsidy is equivalent to the average of the above two percentages: 17.3% of the income of a household living in public housing, irrespective of the type of public housing the household occupies. In other words, the adjusted household income for households living in public housing is derived as:

Adjusted Household Income = Household Income x 1.173.

No adjustment is required for those households living in private housing. For these households, adjusted household income is the same as raw household income. Wong and Liu (1988) clearly point out that this adjustment method provides a benchmark value for assessing the approximate gains to public housing tenants. Moreover, it is incorrect to use this method to study the distribution of benefits among tenants. We are particularly concerned about the benefits received by poor households, and this method assumes a fixed benefit-to-income ratio.[9]

This income adjustment method will overestimate the housing subsidy received by poor tenants. In conclusion, using a constant subsidy-income ratio to compute adjusted income is inappropriate.

Regression Analysis Method

The income ratio method is a rather crude income adjustment method. Aside from the over-estimation and associated problems mentioned in the preceding paragraph in Endnote 9, it does not take into account individual household characteristics. A better method is to include other relevant characteristics about the household and living quarter in deriving the adjusted household income. A simple way to account for household characteristics and living quarter attributes is to employ a regression analysis to estimate monthly rental fees.[10]

I select a sub-sample of households living in private housing and find out the quantitative (regression) relationship between the household income and household size, both adjusted, among the sampled private households. I compute an imputed monthly rental fee for households living in public housing. The imputed rent can be viewed as the amount a public housing tenant would have to pay if he or she lived in private housing. According to this method, the government subsidy received by a household living in public housing is computed as follows:

Subsidy = Imputed Rent – Actual Rent.

Obviously, a government public housing subsidy cannot be negative. If the estimated subsidy is less than zero, the subsidy is set to zero. Finally, the adjusted household income is the sum of household raw income plus government subsidy, i.e.,

Adjusted Household Income = Household Income + Subsidy.

Just as in the income ratio method, no adjustment is required for those households living in private housing. Although I only use two independent variables in this (better) method, the explanatory power of the regression equations model is rather good.[11]

Adjusted Household Income Distribution

Before looking at the distribution of adjusted household income, I present summary characteristics of the distribution of unadjusted household income in Table 4.6. The statistics in the table clearly show that income inequality among households living in public housing blocks is much lower than that of the households in private housing. In 1991 the Gini coefficient for private housing tenants was 36.6% higher than that for public housing tenants, meaning more income inequality among private tenants. In terms of another statistical indicator, the variance of log income, households living in private housing have an income dispersion which was twice of that among public housing tenants.

In the table, I also tabulate the distribution of households by broad housing types.[12]

Over the period 1976 to 1991, the income distribution of Hong Kong households became more uneven; that the rich and the poor

Table 4.6

Decomposition of Income Inequality Distribution by Type of Housing, 1976–1991

(A) % Distribution in Public vs Private Housing

Housing Types	1976	1981	1986	1991
% of Households in				
Public housing	36.6	36.4	42.5	43.8
Private housing	63.4	63.6	57.5	56.2

(B) Income Inequality (Public vs Private Housing)

Gini coefficient				
Public housing	0.372	0.357	0.330	0.358
Private housing	0.475	0.486	0.493	0.488
Overall	0.447	0.452	0.442	0.457

(C) Income Dispersion (variance value)

Variance of log income				
Public housing	0.449	0.559	0.416	0.555
Private housing	0.728	0.901	0.926	1.093
Overall	0.630	0.779	0.710	0.873

(D) Sources of Variance of Income Dispersion

Decomposition of variance				
Between-group variance	0.006	0.004	0.002	0.017
	(1.0)	(0.5)	(0.2)	(1.9)
Within-group variance	0.624	0.775	0.709	0.856
	(99.0)	(99.5)	(99.8)	(98.1)

(E) Analysis of Change of Inequality during 1976–1991

Change in variance (0.873 minus 0.630, from Panel C)	0.243
Due to composition change	−0.039
Between-group	0.000
Within-group	−0.039
Due to change in variance	0.281
Between-group	0.011
Within-group	0.271

Note: Percentage share is in parentheses.

families spread out more widely is measured in terms of "the variance of log household income" which increased by 0.243. In order to better understand this large change in variance, I decompose 0.243 (see Panel E, top row) into two sources of increase in the dispersion of income: the effect of composition change and the effect of change in within-group variance. The lower part of Table 4.6 shows the results of decomposition.

The analysis indicates that the change in variance (rise of inequality) was mainly due to an increase in within-group variance. The change in variance due to the composition change over the period was –0.039. The negative sign points out that composition change (shares of public housing) helped to decrease somewhat the inequality of household income distribution. If the distribution of households by housing type had remained unchanged throughout the period 1976 to 1991, the variance of household income would have increased further, by 0.039 which is a very small effect. At first glance, one may conclude that providing more public housing units seems to slightly reduce the income inequality of households. However, the cause may be due to the system of allocation of public housing flats which follows a rigid predetermined criteria. The selection procedure may account for the apparent reduction of inequality of income distribution among public housing tenants.[13]

A more direct way of assessing the effectiveness of the public housing policy is to analyze adjusted household income distribution. Two income inequality indicators based on the two adjusted household income distributions are presented in Table 4.7. Panel (A) in Table 4.7 refers to the adjusted household income distribution derived from the income ratio method, whereas Panel (B) refers to the adjusted household income distribution estimates (derived from the regression analysis method). Broadly speaking, both methods produce similar results. Most income inequality measure reported in Table 4.7 (A) are slightly lower than the corresponding income inequality estimates in Table 4.6.

As discussed earlier, the income ratio method overestimates the benefits received by poor public housing tenants. The real adjusted

Table 4.7
Adjusted Income Distribution

(A) Income Ratio Method

Indicators of Inequality	1976	1981	1986	1991
Gini coefficient	0.442	0.445	0.434	0.447
Variance of log income	0.626	0.777	0.711	0.860
Decomposition of variance				
Between-group variance	0.000	0.001	0.003	0.002
	(0.0)	(0.1)	(0.4)	(0.2)
Within-group variance	0.626	0.776	0.708	0.858
	(100.0)	(99.9)	(99.6)	(99.8)

(B) Regression Analysis Method

Gini coefficient	0.444	0.449	0.437	0.456
Variance of log income	0.631	0.778	0.704	0.875
Decomposition of variance				
Between-group variance	0.000	0.001	0.000	0.014
	(0.1)	(0.1)	(0.0)	(1.6)
Within-group variance	0.630	0.777	0.704	0.861
	(99.9)	(99.9)	(100.0)	(98.4)

Note: Percentage share is in parentheses.

household income inequality estimates should be higher than those reported in Table 4.7 (A). If we compare the variance of log income in Table 4.7 (A) with the corresponding estimates in Table 3.5 (B), we can see that the reported variances in Table 4.7 (A) are almost equal to those in Table 3.5 (B). This is consistent with Chow and Papanet's (1981) earlier conjecture that the Gini coefficient estimate derived from adjusted income distribution should be close to the official Gini coefficient, even taking into account subsidized public housing in Hong Kong.

Comparing the results in Table 4.7 (A) and Table 4.6, one can see a consistent result that the availability of public housing only marginally reduces income inequality in Hong Kong. Given the massive effort made by the government in building public housing estates, the benefits to tenants were surprisingly small.[14]

In addition to studying the adjusted household income distribution in Table 4.7 (A), we can also analyze the adjusted income distribution in Table 4.7 (B).

Our results show, again, that our public housing programme has very little impact on the distribution of household income. Ironically, the government's housing programme is supposedly aimed at subsidizing poor households with respect to expenditure on housing. If the public housing programme were effective, the income inequality estimates in Table 4.7 would show *much less* inequality in income distribution than would those in Table 3.5 (B). The evidence shows that the programme has not been effective in this regard. Most estimates in panel (B) indicate higher income inequality than do those in panel (A). When we compare the income inequality measures with those in Table 3.5 (B), the differences are negligible. In short, as far as income distribution is concerned, it is unlikely that our public housing programme will be able to achieve its social stability objective.

Beneficiaries of Public Housing

In order to identify the beneficiaries of the public housing pro-gramme, I divide public housing tenants into two groups. Based on the regression analysis method, households that received positive public housing subsidies are classified into one group and all other public housing tenants are classified into another. For the sake of comparison, I also divide private housing tenants into two groups. The first group consists of those families living in rental units, whereas the second group consists of families living in owner-occupied units. The mean household income and mean household size of these four groups of households are presented in Table 4.8. To fulfill its social stability objective, households living in public housing units should have much lower incomes than do those living in the private sector.

As expected, during 1976–1991 tenants living in the public sector had lower incomes than those living in the private sector. The average household size of public housing tenants was larger than was that of their private sector counterparts. This is partly because

Table 4.8
Characteristics of Public and Private Housing Tenants

(A) Public Housing Rental Units

Variables	1976	1981	1986	1991
Units with subsidy				
Household income	1,728	3,434	5,667	11,961
Household size	5.19	4.80	4.17	3.87
Units without subsidy				
Household income	904	1,717	3,666	5,425
Household size	4.55	5.19	5.25	4.02
% of Housing				
With subsidy	93.4	90.7	97.9	69.8
Without subsidy	6.6	9.3	2.1	30.2

(B) Private Housing

Rental units				
Household income	1,918	3,756	6,989	14,493
Household size	3.35	3.25	2.85	2.63
Owner-occupied units				
Household income	2,520	5,211	8,923	18,282
Household size	4.46	4.14	3.66	3.38

Calculations are based on 1% census files.

newly married couples are unlikely to be allocated a public housing unit; the household sizes of these families were relatively small. If we focus on the public sector, the household size of tenants with subsidies were larger than were those of tenants without subsidies.

A striking piece of information presented in Table 4.8 is that the mean household income of households with subsidies was substantially higher than was that of those without subsidies. In 1976, mean income of those with subsidies was HK$1,728 per month, compared to HK$904 for those without. So, the income ratio of households with subsidies to households without subsidies was 1.9 in 1976. This ratio increased to 2.2 in 1991 (HK$11,961 vs HK$5,425 per month). This finding is consistent with the results of Wong and Liu's (1988) study. They argue that inefficiencies arise because some families are forced to consume too much housing, while others spend too little. Wong and Liu also point out that rich families reduced their housing consumption, whereas poor house-holds raised their expenditure on housing. These figures suggest that poor tenants were spending more on housing than were those households in the private sector, after controlling for other independent variables. On the other hand, rich public housing tenants were forced to consume less housing than those living in private rental units.

The average household income of families living in private rental units was just 10% higher than that of public housing tenants with subsidies in 1976. This income ratio increased to 1.2 (or 20% higher) in 1991. This private-public income ratio could be still lower if another factor is taken into consideration. Given that some families living in private rental units are very rich, and that most senior civil servants or senior managers and professionals in the private sector enjoy fairly high housing subsidies from their employers, if we remove these relatively few but very well-off families from the sample, the average income of families living in private rental units would be quite a bit lower. It is therefore likely that their resulting average household income is very close to that of tenants receiving public housing subsidies.

Given that their average income is about the same, it is doubtful that we should subsidize well-off families living in public housing for reasons of either equity or efficiency. All of the above points support our conclusion that the distribution of public housing benefits is highly uneven. As so much of the taxpayers' money goes towards public housing, and as the resulting benefits of public housing are so minimal, the government should seriously consider revamping the public housing programme.

Notes

1. I thank Salween Wong of the Finance Branch, Government Secretariat, for drawing my attention to this point.

2. In Hong Kong and in the U.K. a "graduate" is a person who holds a *university* degree, especially a first (bachelor's) degree. In North America, the term graduate refers to a person who has completed his or her studies in an educational institution.

3. The technical procedure in estimating the income ratios are as follows: After running an earning regression, I subtract the coefficient estimate of an education dummy by the coefficient estimate of a secondary school dummy. The income ratio is computed by taking the exponential of the difference in coefficient estimates. The interpretation of the resulting income ratio is very straightforward and can be interpreted in the same way in which income ratio is computed from raw income.

4. The procedure to analyze the income dispersion within and between the educational groups are as follows: I attempt to decompose the changes in inequality of income distribution into two major components. In particular, I want to study the changes in within-group variance and the changes in between-group variance. Table 4.5 summarizes the variance of log income by educational level. I also compute the overall variance and the between-group or within-group variance. In order to explain the contribution of between-group variance and within-group variance, Table 4.5 shows their respective percentage shares in parentheses.

5. If we study the overall composition, we can see that income dispersion within education groups accounts for the bulk of the overall variance. Moreover, the percentage share of between-group variance, i.e. income dispersion between different education groups, increased from 20.7% to 22.4%. In the period 1976 to 1991, the variance of logarithmic income increased by 22%, from 0.398 in 1976 to 0.484 in 1991. I decompose the rise in variance into two major components, change in composition and change in variance. The results are presented in Table 4.5.

6. Readers who are interested in the development of the public housing programme in Hong Kong can consult Fong's (1980) doctoral dissertation and the annual departmental reports of the Housing Authority and former Resettlement Department. Fong's dissertation focuses on identifying key factors to explain why the public housing programme in Hong Kong was so successful, whereas other developing countries have been unable to alleviate housing problems similar to the one that existed in Hong Kong. Fung (1996) provides a brief overview of the past, present, and future of the public housing policy in Hong Kong. In recent years, the government has intended to convert some public housing

rental units into owner-occupied units. Ho (1995) discusses alternative privatization schemes for public housing.

7. A technical note on Wu's incorrect estimates. Wu (1973) makes use of published 1971 census statistics to calculate the total subsidies in public housing by income group. The total subsidies by income group are then added to the estimated total income of each income group to obtain an adjusted income distribution. The Gini coefficient estimated by using his adjusted income distribution was 0.74 in 1971, as compared to the official estimate of 0.43. In his calculations, the public housing subsidy per household for the highest income group is 97 times that of the lowest income group. If we look at the absolute value, the subsidy to the highest income group is HK$877, which is 6.6 times their average rent. I agree with Chow and Papanet (1981) that Wu's calculations are incorrect.

8. A side point about the quality of public versus private housing. If we view the difference in rental charge as a subsidy, we implicitly assume that all aspects of private and public housing rental units, except for the rental charge, are equivalent. However, one may argue that the living conditions in public housing estates are not as good as are those in the private sector. Fong (1980) compares the facilities and living conditions of public and private housing. He uses a number of measurements, such as degree of overcrowding, piped water supply, toilet, and kitchen, to assess the living conditions in public and private housing. He argues that private tenement blocks are often as bad as or worse than are public housing estates. It therefore seems reasonable to assume that the difference in average rental charge is a kind of government transfer. As discussed in Chapter 3, total household income should also include this kind of government subsidy.

9. Notes on the effects of selection rules in public housing allocation. Even when the living conditions in public housing estates are the same as are those in the private sector, public housing tenants have no freedom to make their own choices in relation to location, size, facilities, rent etc. For example, rent is directly related to the size, the location, and the facilities of the rental unit concerned. The Housing Authority allocates rental flats to tenants according to its own criteria, which includes household size, seniority on the waiting list, and current standard area per person.

As long as household income falls below the stipulated maximum at the time of a household's admission into the public housing programme, household income itself doesn't come into play in the allocation of a flat. In the private sector, affordability is one of the prime determinants in making any housing choice. The income ceiling rule only applies at the point at which a household joins the housing programme. Once a tenant has been accepted into the programme, income exceeding the stipulated maximum has no effect on his or her status, except that he or she may be subject to higher rental fees after having been in the programme for ten years or more. It is commonly known that a significant portion of public housing tenants own private property. It is highly likely that new tenants pay a much higher rental-to-income ratio than do old tenants.

10. Generally, people expect rent to be closely related to the characteristics of a living space, such as its size, its location, its facilities, and its surrounding environment. Unfortunately, the census files used in this study do not contain detailed living quarter information. From the viewpoint of a tenant, affordability is the prime determinant in choosing a suitable flat.

11. A note on sample bias and the quality of estimation by the regression method. The statistical criterion used to evaluate the procedure is "R-squared". The adjusted R-squared value is around 0.3, which suggests that the independent variables used explain about 30% of the variance of the dependent variable. The possible shortcomings of this regression procedure are as follows: This sample of households living in private rental units is unlikely to be a random one. Some of the households may prefer to live in public housing but may not be eligible to apply for public housing for different reasons; for example, the duration of their residence in Hong Kong may be too short, or their household income may be too high. Other households are eligible to apply and are on the waiting list. The Housing Authority's rationing exercises create a sample selection bias. Furthermore, the provision of public housing on the scale at which it exists in Hong Kong may distort the market price of private housing when there are no government-subsidized flats available. Using the rental equation for private housing tenants to impute monthly rental fees for public housing tenants may be subject to this kind of sample selection bias. Bearing this in mind, the empirical results that follow are very crude estimates of the real situation. However, I believe that these problems should only affect the magnitude and not the direction of the empirical estimates.

12. Despite the massive influx of Chinese immigrants into Hong Kong in the past, the Hong Kong government managed to accommodate more than one-third of all households in public housing estates in 1976. When the government tightened the immigration policy in the late 1970s, the inflow of Chinese immigrants was largely under control. The percentage share of households living in public housing gradually increased from 35.6% in 1976 to 43.8% in 1991. By 1995, 3.2 million people, or 51% of the population, lived in various types of subsidized housing (Information Services Department 1996b).

13. If we decompose the variance of log household income, we can see that the dispersion of household income in the four census years was due to within-group variances. The between-group variance explains less than 2% of the variance of log household income.

14. Wong and Liu (1988) show that the benefits to public housing tenants were substantially below the reported public expenditure on housing.

Based on a 1% random sample of the 1981 census, they estimate that the value of housing services is around 60% of total public expenditure on the public housing programme. In other words, the amount of the subsidies is much higher than are the benefits enjoyed by public housing tenants.

CHAPTER 5

Summary and Conclusions

"Equality is a luxury of rich societies. If poor societies are to maintain any kind of peak achievement or civilization, they simply cannot afford it."

Kenneth E. Boulding (1962)

Summary

The economy of Hong Kong has been developing at a rapid pace in the last three decades. The real GDP per capita increased 5.3 times between 1961 and 1995. The growth of the population and the working population was equally impressive. The population increased by 3 million people, and the labour force gained 1.7 million workers. That Hong Kong has undergone economic restructuring is an often-told story. The economy successfully developed from an entrepôt to a manufacturing economy and by now to a service economy. Labour-intensive manufacturing industries have shifted their production plants to Mainland China. The number of employed persons in the manufacturing sector dropped from 990,000 in 1981 to 768,000 in 1991. Today the service sector dominates the labour market, employing more than 60% of the domestic workforce. Within the service sector, wholesale and retail trade, restaurants, and hotels, as well as financing, insurance, real estate, and business services account for most of the rise in employment.

There is a general belief that large-scale sectoral shifts lead to substantial changes in relative earnings; and that changes in industrial composition is the major factor responsible for the overall rise in income inequality in Hong Kong, especially for the

105

period 1976–1991. However, sectoral shifts have had a minimal effect on the rise of income dispersion in more recent years (1986–1991). Empirical results indicate that Hong Kong workers are relatively mobile across industries.

Many researchers use the Gini coefficient as the only indicator of inequality of income distribution. Unfortunately, the Gini coefficient and some other frequently used income inequality measurements are sometimes abused or misused. In Chapter 3, I discuss the commonly used measures of income inequality, including the Gini coefficient and the variance of log income, and I describe the desirable properties that an income inequality measure should possess. A general description of the data sets used in this study is included in the same chapter.

The working population as a whole has been better educated in recent years than it was in the past. When the government abolished the "reach base" repatriation policy of illegal immigrants in October 1980, the inflow of Chinese immigrants into Hong Kong was brought under the control. Hence, the percentage of Chinese immigrant workers in the total workforce dropped from 53.6% in 1976 to 35.1% in 1991. The composition of the workforce also reflects the increasing internationalization of Hong Kong's economy. Foreign workers accounted for 6.6% of the country's labour force in 1991, as compared to 3.2% in 1976.

As Hong Kong prospers, its labour market moves towards greater income distribution inequality. At the same time when the Gini coefficient increased from 0.377 in 1976 to 0.421 in 1991, the variance of log income rose 22% in the same period. Analysis shows that the gender-earnings gap was significant and pervasive during 1976–1991. Moreover, the distribution of main employment income of females was less unequal than that of males. During the period, Hong Kong's average household size declined.

If we were to focus only on the Gini coefficient of household income distribution, we might conclude that the income inequality situation remained more or less the same throughout the period 1976–1991. However, the variance of log household income increased from 0.630 to 0.873 in the same period, which indicates that the household income became more unequal among Hong Kong households as a whole. The sources of this rise in the dispersion of household income are identified in Chapter 4.

In Chapter 3, I also take a closer look at the socioeconomic characteristics of natives and Chinese immigrants. As expected, Hong Kong born workers were much younger and better educated than the immigrants from China. Although native workers earned more, their income distribution was more unequal than that among Chinese immigrants.

Undoubtedly, public policy has a major impact on the distribution of personal as well as of household income. In this study, I analyze the relations between income distribution and the education policy and the public housing policy.

Inequality Induced by Education

An international comparison shows that the percentage of public spending on education in Hong Kong is rather low. The territory spent less than 3% of its GDP on education in 1990, which was much less than the corresponding figure for other developing and industrialized economies such as Korea (4.2%), Japan (4.7%), the U.S. (5.3%), and Canada (6.8%). However, if we compare the percentage share of public spending on education, Hong Kong ranks rather high on the international scale. Public spending on education consistently accounts for about 17% of total public expenditure in Hong Kong, making it the largest single item on the government budget. In fact, the Hong Kong government is strongly committed to the education system.

The provision of better educational opportunities and to a higher quality of teaching and learning at all levels has proved beneficial to Hong Kong's economy. Despite the marked shifts in labour demand caused by rapid economic transformation, income growth rates across different educational levels were in the same order of magnitude. The increasing supply of better-educated workers in the labour market has allowed Hong Kong's economic restructuring to proceed rather smoothly. On the other hand, income dispersion has increased among those better-educated workers during 1976–1991. My analysis indicates that the changing *composition* of our workforce in terms of educational attainment accounts for most of the increase in income dispersion. The implication is that, other things being equal, the expansion of tertiary education in Hong Kong has led, and will lead, to heightened inequality in income distribution.

Inequality Induced by Public Housing

Since the inception of the public housing programme in 1954, the Hong Kong government has invested heavily in various types of public housing. In 1995 about half the population, or 3.2 million people, lived in government-subsidized housing. Households living in public housing are required to pay rents much lower than the market price. In this study, I use two income adjustment methods to account for the amount of public housing subsidies. The results show that government subsidies in the form of reduced rent paid by households living in public housing do not materially change the overall inequality of household income distribution. The distribution of benefits among tenants is highly uneven. Well-off families living in public housing are paying too little rent (relative to their high income), or to express it in economics terms, "forced to consume less housing". Conversely, poor families in public housing are paying too much, or "forced to consume too much housing". As far as income distribution is concerned, the public housing programme has failed to achieve its social stability objective. The government should take a hard look at the costs and benefits of the public housing programme.

Suggestions for Future Research

In this book, I limit my attention to the education policy and the public housing policy, and to their relationship with income distribution. Many other public policy issues are not considered here. For example, Hong Kong's taxation policy, which directly affects disposable income, has been left out because of a data availability problem. Also left out are social welfare and social security policies that mainly cater for the poor and disadvantaged; these are public vehicles that address income inequality issues. Moreover, the immigration policy in general and the policy on immigration from China in particular should be studied carefully. In order to study these issues, a suitable data set would be needed.

In this book, I attempt to derive an adjusted household income distribution by using two simple income adjustment methods to account for public housing subsidies received by tenants. These methods are rather crude and do not take into account the differences in types of public housing. A more sophisticated method coupled with a richer data set is required to address the problem efficiently and effectively. Census files made available to researchers by the government are the most comprehensive data sources available in Hong Kong so far. Unfortunately, the population census and most conventional large-scale surveys do not contain enough information for more in-depth studies of the relationship between public policy and income distribution. If the government wants to seriously address the income inequality problem, it will need to conduct a dedicated survey to collect the relevant information.

Concluding Remarks

When Hong Kong developed from an entrepôt into a service economy, the distribution of labour and household income became more uneven. The interrelation between economic growth and income inequality is still an unresolved puzzle. Nonetheless, Becker (1995) argues that greater income inequality may be an engine that drives an economy toward more rapid economic growth. Hong Kong's experience seems to support his view. Boulding (1962) suggests too that when poor societies have to maintain their economic growth, "(income) equality is a luxury"; in other words, income inequality is an inevitable fact.

Public policy may have major impact on income dispersion; but as reflected by the analytical results of this book, the outcome may be ironic and even counter-intuitive. Providing more and better educational opportunities to the Hong Kong people was well supported by the changing economic environment, but it also *increased* income dispersion. Providing more public housing is another ironic example: It has had a negligible impact on income distribution. These conclusions are of major political importance because, whatever the reasons might be, inadvertent increases in the level of inequality in income distribution may lead to heightened social tension. Although this book does not provide a comprehensive analysis of all the relations between public policies and the distribution of labour and household income in Hong Kong, its key conclusions should help the government and the general public to re-assess the effects of present public policies of education and public housing on income distribution.

Bibliography

1. Adelman, Irma and Sherman Robinson (1989). "Income Distribution and Development." In Hollis Chenery and T. N. Srinivasan (eds.) *Handbook of Development Economics*. Volume 2. Amsterdam: North Holland.

2. Anand, Sudhir and S. M. R. Kanbur (1993). "The Kuznets Process and the Inequality-Development Relationship." *Journal of Development Economics* 40: 215–52.

3. Becker, Gary S. (1995). "Maybe the Earnings Gap Isn't Such a Bad Thing." *Business Week*, 6 Febraury 1995, p. 24.

4. Birdsall, Nancy, David Ross and Richard Sabot (1995). "Inequality and Growth Reconsidered: Lessons from East Asia." *The Word Bank Economic Review* 9: 477–508.

5. Blau, Francine D. and Lawrence M. Kahn (1992). "The Gender Earnings Gap: Learning from International Comparisons." *American Economic Review* 82: 533–538.

6. _____ (1996). "International Differences in Male Wage Inequality: Institutions versus Market Forces." *Journal of Political Economy* 104: 791–837.

7. Bluestone, Barry (1990). "The Impact of Schooling and Industrial Restructuring on Recent Trends in Wage Inequality in the United States."*American Economic Review* 80: 303–307.

8. Borjas, George J. (1990). *Friends or Strangers: The Impact of Immigrants on the US Economy*. New York: Basic Books.

9. Boulding, Kenneth E. (1962). "Social Justice in Social Dynamics." In Richard R. Brandt (ed.) *Social Justice*. Englewood Cliffs, N.J.: Prentice-Hall.

10. Browning, Edgar K. (1989). "Inequality and Poverty." *Southern Economic Journal* 55: 819–830.

11. Caldwell, John C. (1982). *Theory of Fertility Decline*. New York: Academic Press.

12. Census & Statistics Department (1978). *Hong Kong By-Census 1976: Main Report*. Volume 1. Hong Kong: Government Printer.

13. _____ (1993). *Hong Kong 1991 Population Census: Main Report*. Hong Kong: Government Printer.

14. _____ (1995). *Hong Kong Annual Digest of Statistics: 1995*. Hong Kong: Government Printer.

15. _____ (1996a). *Estimates of Gross Domestic Product: 1961 to 1995*. Hong Kong: Government Printer.

16. _____ (1996b). *Hong Kong in Figures — 1996 Edition*. Hong Kong: Government Printer.

17. _____ (1996c). *Hong Kong Monthly Digest of Statistics: December 1996*. Hong Kong: Government Printer.

18. Chang, Roberto (1994). "Income Inequality and Economic Growth: Evidence and Recent Theories." *Federal Reserve Bank of Atlanta Economic Review* 79: 1–10.

19. Chau, L. C. (1994). "Economic Growth and Income Distribution in Hong Kong." In Benjamin K. P. Leung and Teresa Y. C. Wong (eds.) *25 Years of Social and Economic Development in Hong Kong*. Centre of Asian Studies Occasional Papers and books No. 111, The University of Hong Kong.

20. Chen, Edward K. Y. (1979). *Hyper-growth in Asian Economies*. London: Macmillan.

21. Chow, Steven Chi-Man (1977). Economic Growth and Income Distribution in Hong Kong. PhD Dissertation, Boston University.

22. _____ and Gustav F. Papanek (1981). "Laissez-Faire, Growth and Equity — Hong Kong." *Economic Journal* 91: 466–485.

23. Coale, Ansley J. and Susan Cotts Watkins (eds.) (1986). *The Decline of Fertility in Europe: The Revised Proceedings of a Conference on the Princeton European Fertility Project*. Princeton, N.J.: Princeton University Press.

24. Cole, J. and C. Towe (1996). "Income Distribution and Macroeconomic Performance in the United States." Working Paper of the International Monetary Fund.

25. Cowell, Frank A. (1995). *Measuring Inequality*. Second Edition. Hertfordshire, U.K.: Prentice Hall/Harvester Wheatsheaf.

26. Danziger, Sheldon (1980). "Do Working Wives Increase Family Income Inequality?" *Journal of Human Resources* 15: 444–451.

27. Davis, Kingsley, Mikhail S. Bernstam and Rita Ricardo-Campell (eds.) (1987). *Below Replacement Fertility in Industrial Societies: Causes, Consequences, Policies.* New York: Cambridge University Press.

28. Deininger, Klaus and Lyn Squire (1996). "A New Data Set Measuring Income Inequality." *The World Bank Economic Review* 10: 565–591.

29. Fan, Shuh Ching (1974). *The Population of Hong Kong.* Hong Kong: Swindon Book Co., Ltd.

30. Fong, Peter K. W. (1980). Housing Problems and Public Housing Program in Hong Kong: A Case Study of the Housing Provision in a Densely Populated Metropolitan Area. PhD dissertation, New York University, 1980.

31. Fung, Tung (1996). The Housing Challenge Ahead: Hong Kong. URL = http://www.info.gov.hk/hd/housconf/dhspeech.htm. May 1996.

32. Green, Gordon, John Coder and Paul Ryscavage (1992). "International Comparisons of Earnings Inequality for Men in the 1980s." *Review of Income and Wealth* 38: 1–15.

33. Greenwood, John (1990). "The Changing Structure and Competitiveness of the Hong Kong Economy." *Asian Monetary Monitor* 14: 21–31.

34. Grubb, W. Norton and Robert H. Wilson (1989). "Sources of Increasing Inequality in Wages and Salaries, 1960–80." *Monthly Labor Review* 112: 3–13.

35. Gunderson, Morley (1989). "Male-Female Wage Differentials and Policy Responses." *Journal of Economic Literature* 27: 25–41.

36. Hamermesh, Daniel S. and Albert Rees (1993). *The Economics of Work and Pay.* Fifth Edition. New York: Harper Collins College Publishers.

37. Haslag, Joseph H., Thomas B. Fomby and D. J. Slottje (1988). "A Study of the Relationship between Economic Growth and Inequality: The Case of Mexico." *Federal Reserve Bank of Dallas Economic Review*: 13–25.

38. Hayes, Kathy and Daniel J. Slottje (1989). "The Efficacy of State and Local Governments' Redistributional Policies." *Public Finance Quarterly* 17: 304–322.

39. Heckman, James J. (1979). "Sample Selection as a Specification Error." *Econometrica* 47: 153–161.

40. Ho, H. C. Y. (1979). *The Fiscal System in Hong Kong.* London: Croom Helm.

41. Ho, Lok-Sang (1995). "Privatization of Public Housing: An Analysis of Policy Alternatives." *Contemporary Economic Policy* 13: 53–63.

42. _____, Pak-Wai Liu and Kit-Chun Lam (1991). "International Labour Migration: The Case of Hong Kong." Occasional Paper No. 8, Hong Kong Institute of Asia-Pacific Studies, The Chinese University of Hong Kong.

43. Howell, David R. (1995). "Collapsing Wages and Rising Inequality: Has Computerization Shifted the Demand for Skills?" *Challenge* 38: 27–35.

44. Hsia, Ronald and Laurence Chau (1978). *Industrialisation, Employment and Income Distribution: A Case Study of Hong Kong*. London: Croom Helm.

45. Information Services Department, Hong Kong Government (1996a). URL = http:// www.info.gov.hk/info/education.htm. 1 September 1996.

46. _____ (1996b). URL=http://www.info.gov.hk/info/housing.htm. July 1996.

47. _____ (1996c). URL=http://www.info.gov.hk/info/schs.htm. July 1996.

48. Jenkins, Stephen P. (1995). "Accounting for Inequality Trends: Decomposition Analysis for the UK: 1971–86." *Economica* 62: 29–63.

49. Johnson, Paul and Steven Webb (1993). "Explaining the Growth in UK Income Inequality: 1979–1988." *Economic Journal* 103: 429–435.

50. Juhn, Chinhui, Kevin M. Murphy and Brooks Pierce (1993). "Wage Inequality and the Rise in Returns to Skill." *Journal of Political Economy* 101: 410–442.

51. Katz, Lawrence F. and Ana L. Ravenga (1989). "Changes in the Structure of Wages: The United States vs. Japan." *Journal of the Japanese and International Economy* 3: 522–554.

52. Killingsworth, Mark R. (1983). *Labor Supply*. New York: Cambridge University Press.

53. King, Mervyn A. (1980). "How Effective Have Fiscal Policies Been in Changing the Distribution of Income and Wealth?" *American Economic Review* 70: 72–76.

54. Kuznets, Simon (1955). "Economic Growth and Income Inequality." *American Economic Review* 45: 1–28.

55. Lam, Kit–Chun (1995). "Immigration and Income Distribution in Hong Kong." Working Paper, Hong Kong Baptist University, June 1995.

56. Lawrence, Robert Z. (1984). "Sectoral Shifts and the Size of the Middle Class." *Brookings Review* 3: 3–11.

57. Leonard, Jonathan S. and Louis Jocobson (1990). "Earnings Inequality and Job Turnover." *American Economic Review* 80: 298–302.

58. Levy, Frank and Richard J. Murnane (1992). "U.S. Earnings Levels and Earnings Inequality: A Review of Recent Trends and Proposed Explanations." *Journal of Economic literature* 30: 1333–1381.

59. Lin, Tzong-Biau (1985). "Growth, Equity, and Income Distribution Policies in Hong Kong." *The Developing Economies* 23: 391–413.

60 _____ and Chyau Tuan (eds.) (1993). *The Asian NIEs: Success and Challenge*. Hong Kong: Lo Fung Learned Society.

61. Lowe, Vivien Hoh (1980). Family Structure and Fertility in Hong Kong. PhD Dissertation, University of Wisconsin at Madison.

62. Lui, Hon-Kwong (1994). "The Expansion of Tertiary Education in Hong Kong: An Economic Perspective." *Higher Education Review* 27: 23–33.

63. Lui, Hon-Kwong and Wing Suen (1993). "The Narrowing Gender Gap in Hong Kong: 1976–1986." *Asian Economic Journal* VII: 167–180.

64. _____ (1994). "The structure of the Female Earnings Gap in Hong Kong." *Hong Kong Economic Papers* 23: 15–29.

65. _____ (1996). "Does School Quality Matter? Evidence from the Hong Kong Experience." Working Paper, May 1996.

66. Mincer, Jacob (1970). "The Distribution of Labor Incomes: A Survey with Special Reference to the Human Capital Approach." *Journal of Economic Literature* 8: 1–26.

67. _____ (1974). *Schooling, Experience, and Earnings*. New York: National Bureau of Economic Research.

68. Mok, Victor (1993). *The Development and Structural Change of the Hong Kong Economy*. Hong Kong: Joint Publishing.

69. Newbery, David M. (1995). "The Distributional Impact of Price Changes in Hungary and the United Kingdom." *Economic Journal* 105: 847–863.

70. Nickell, Stephen and Brian Bell (1996). "Changes in the Distribution of Wages and Unemployment in OECD Countries." *American Economic Review* 86: 302–308.

71. O'Neill, Dave M. (1984). "The Quiet Revolution in Education Attainment." *Challenge* 27: 57–61.

72. Oshima, Harry T. (1987). *Economic Growth in Monsoon Asia: A Comparative Survey*. Tokyo: University of Tokyo Press.

73. Persson, Torten and Guido Tabellini (1994). "Is Inequality Harmful for Growth?" *American Economic Review* 84: 600–621.

74. Pong, Suet-Ling (1989). Marital Fertility and Family Income Inequality in Hong Kong: Consequences of Women's Employment and Education. PhD Dissertation, University of Chicago.

75. Rosenfeld, Rachel A. and Arne L. Kalleberg (1990). "A Cross-National Comparison of the Gender Gap in Income." *American Journal of Sociology* 96: 96–106.

76. Sahota, Gian S. (1978). "Theories of Personal Income Distribution: A Survey." *Journal of Economic Literature* 16: 1–55.

77. Simon, Julian L. (1989). *The Economic Consequences of Immigration*. Cambridge, Mass.: Basil Blackwell.

78. Siu, Yat-Ming (1988). Family Structure, Marriage and Fertility in Hong Kong: Demographic Effects of the Changing Chinese Family. PhD Dissertation, University of Michigan, 1988.

79. Smith, James P. (1979). "The Distribution of Family Earnings." *Journal of Political Economy* 87: S163–S192.

80. Stark, Oded (1991). *The Migration of Labor*. Cambridge, Mass.: Blackwell Publishers.

81. Suen, Wing (1994). "Market-Procured Housework: The Demand for Domestic Servants and Female Labor Supply." *Labour Economics* 1: 289–302.

82. _____ (1995). "Sectoral Shifts: Impact on Hong Kong Workers." *The Journal of International Trade & Development* 4: 135–152.

83. Tilak, Jandhyala B.G. (1994). *Education for Development in Asia*. Delhi: Sage Publications India Pvt. Ltd.

84. Tsang, Shu-Ki (1993). "Income Distribution." In Choi Po-King and Ho Lok-Sang (Eds.) *The Other Hong Kong Report 1993*. Hong Kong: The Chinese University Press.

85. Tsui, Kai-Yuen (1992). "Multidimensional Generalizations of the Relative and Absolute Inequality Indices: the Atkinson-Kolm-Sen Approach." Working Paper No. 18, Department of Economics, Chinese University of Hong Kong.

86. UNESCO (1995). *Statistical Yearbook*. 1995 Edition. Paris: UNESCO.

87. Vanhoudt, Patrick (1996). "Inequality, Labor Market Policies and Economic Growth: Is There a Connection? Empirical Evidence for the OECD Countries." Working Paper of the International Monetary Fund, September, 1996.

88. Wise, David A. (ed.) (1990). *Issues in the Economics of Aging*. Chicago: University of Chicago Press.

89. _____. (ed.) (1992). *Topics in the Economics of Aging*. Chicago: University of Chicago Press.

90. _____. (ed.) (1994). *Studies in the Economics of Aging*. Chicago: University of Chicago Press.

91. Wong, Richard Y. C., Liu Pak-Wai and Alan K. F. Siu (1991). *Inflation in Hong Kong: Patterns, Causes and Policies*. Hong Kong: Business and Professional Federation of Hong Kong, 1991.

92. Wong, Yue-Chim (1981). Family, Work Status and Earnings Distribution in Hong Kong. PhD Dissertation, University of Chicago, 1981.

93. _____ and Pak-Wai Liu (1988). "The Distribution of Benefits Among Public Housing Tenants in Hong Kong and Related Policy Issues." *Journal of Urban Economics* 23: 1–20.

94. World Bank (1995). *World Development Report 1995: Workers in an Integrating World*. New York: Oxford University Press.

95. Wu, Chung-Tong (1973). Societal Guidance and Development: A Case Study of Hong Kong. PhD Dissertation, University of California, Los Angeles, 1973.

96. Young, Alwyn (1992). "A Tale of Two Cities: Factor Accumulation and Technical Change in Hong Kong and Singapore." *NBER Macroeconomics Annual* 7: 13–54.

Index

About the Author

LUI Hon-Kwong received his BSc(Econ) from the University of London, and the MSocSc and PhD degrees from the University of Hong Kong. He is Assistant Professor in the Department of Marketing and International Business at Lingnan College. Dr. Lui was previously Statistician of the Census & Statistics Department of the Hong Kong Government. Before joining the civil service, he was a marketing executive of a fashion retail chain. His research interests focus on the economics of human behaviour.

The Hong Kong Economic Policy Studies Series